New Directions for
Higher Education

Martin Kramer and
Betsy Barefoot
CO-EDITORS-IN-CHIEF

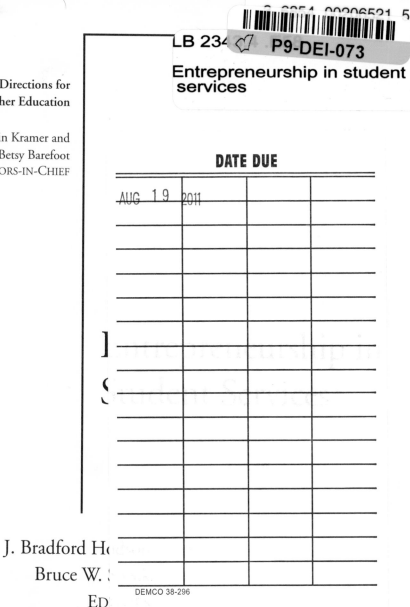

J. Bradford H

Bruce W.

ED

Number 153 • Spring 2011
Jossey-Bass
San Francisco

ENTREPRENEURSHIP IN STUDENT SERVICES
*J. Bradford Hodson and Bruce W. Speck*
New Directions for Higher Education, no. 153
*Martin Kramer, Betsy Barefoot,* Co-Editors-in-Chief

Microfilm copies of issues and articles are available in 16mm and 35mm, as well as microfiche in 105mm, through University Microfilms Inc., 300 North Zeeb Road, Ann Arbor, MI 48106-1346.

NEW DIRECTIONS FOR HIGHER EDUCATION (ISSN 0271-0560, electronic ISSN 1536-0741) is part of The Jossey-Bass Higher and Adult Education Series and is published quarterly by Wiley Subscription Services, Inc., A Wiley Company, at Jossey-Bass, 989 Market Street, San Francisco, CA 94103-1741. Periodicals Postage Paid at San Francisco, California, and at additional mailing offices. POSTMASTER: Send address changes to New Directions for Higher Education, Jossey-Bass, 989 Market Street, San Francisco, CA 94103-1741.

*New Directions for Higher Education* is indexed in Current Index to Journals in Education (ERIC); Higher Education Abstracts.

SUBSCRIPTIONS cost $89 for individuals and $259 for institutions, agencies, and libraries. See ordering information page at end of journal.

EDITORIAL CORRESPONDENCE should be sent to the Co-Editors-in-Chief, Martin Kramer, 2807 Shasta Road, Berkeley, CA 94708-2011 and Betsy Barefoot, Gardner Institute, Box 72, Brevard, NC 28712.

Cover photograph © Digital Vision

www.josseybass.com

# CONTENTS

# EDITORS' NOTES

Student affairs professionals serve an important purpose in American higher education. Not only do they attempt to provide personal attention to a student's social, physical, and psychological needs, but they also promote student learning through out-of-classroom activities and environments that help each student develop a sense of belonging in the campus community.

The professional arena of student affairs is comprised of many diverse programs and offices, but all with a common purpose: to provide personal support so that students can achieve academic success. Common offices within student affairs include campus activities, health and counseling services, residence life, enrollment management, the student center, recreation and intramurals, dining services, Greek life, and student conduct and discipline. Each campus will have its own unique organizational structure for student affairs, but the common thread is still to provide support to all other student needs, often in concert with academic affairs.

Often led by a vice president or vice chancellor of student affairs or some other organizational iteration, the offices and programs that comprise the student affairs function on any campus are committed in engaging students in learning that supports the classroom experience. Often this includes the development of values and ethical standards; enhanced written, verbal, and organizational skills; improved social and interpersonal skills; and the development of a personal commitment to the university and student communities on campus and off. Whether it is engaging students in Greek life, a residence hall study group, campus activities, or any other student affairs–related program or service, the aim is to continue the students' learning outside the classroom in a way that ultimately supports the learning within the academy.

To that end, a review of how a handful of American colleges and universities are addressing current issues in student affairs will be helpful to professionals as they work to develop new and innovative programming to assist students in the pursuit of personal and intellectual excellence throughout their higher education experience.

## Purpose of This Volume

How are leaders in American higher education addressing current issues in student affairs such as student wellness, veterans' affairs, transfer students, information technology, etc.? This was the question that launched this volume. With so many new issues emerging in the area of student affairs because of changing student demographics, demand for greater accountability, and the emergence of new technology, a volume putting forth some possible solutions to those issues seemed appropriate. Hence the purpose

NEW DIRECTIONS FOR HIGHER EDUCATION, no. 153, Spring 2011 © Wiley Periodicals, Inc.
Published online in Wiley Online Library (wileyonlinelibrary.com) • DOI: 10.1002/he.419

of this volume is to share with readers the perspectives of those in student affairs who have addressed these issues and developed a body of knowledge from those experiences. The information contained within this book is intended to provide practical advice and information to presidents, deans, and student affairs professionals. The goal in creating this volume was to offer some "out of the box" solutions to today's most pressing student affairs issues.

## Overview of the Volume

Authors who have experience with entrepreneurial student affairs programs in higher education have written the eight chapters in this volume. They offer their own unique perspectives on the particular topic they address in their respective chapter. Topics were selected from discussion between the editors as to what were some of the cutting-edge programs in student affairs today. The information contained in this volume is not intended to be highly theoretical because the editors intend for the information contained within to be practical and applicable. Readers should find immediate "take-aways" from the chapters, information they can use to address issues on their own campus.

Taken as a whole, this volume offers a great variety of information on topics of current interest to presidents, provosts, deans, and other leaders of the academy. For instance, with the United States involved in a war on two fronts, Iraq and Afghanistan, a growing number of military and veteran students are enrolling in colleges and universities. Understanding the unique issues that face these students, assisting them in accessing the unique benefits available to them through the federal government, and offering counseling, health, and social services to the veteran students and their families in an effort to increase retention and graduate rates are some of the many challenges facing student affairs professionals today. This volume attempts to address these types of practical issues.

## Overview of the Chapters

In Chapter One, "The Course Concierge Service," Paul Neill outlines how students facing enrollment challenges are assisted by an individual known as the "Course Concierge." This individual assisted students, mostly juniors and seniors, with resolving difficult course schedules, gaining admission into closed classes, and negotiating prerequisite courses in the later years of their degree program. As the service became more popular, patterns of needs were identified that allowed the concierge service to focus on common needs, thereby making the service of value to even more students. Designed to keep students on track to graduate in four years, the service supplements the traditional academic advisor, stepping in when students are unable to resolve issues themselves. Neill describes how the concierge service has helped his institution handle fewer course offerings in recent years due to the nation's economic crisis that has affected higher education.

In Chapter Two, "Rendezvous with the World: Missouri Southern State University's Themed Semesters," Chad Stebbins recounts how the university used a themed semester to capitalize on the institution's mission in international education. Unlike international travel that only benefits the individual experiencing the culture of another country, the themed semester has brought international speakers, food, music, and art to MSSU's campus and impacted faculty, students, and the community as a whole. Stebbins described how a country or region of the world is selected for inclusion in the themed semester program, how events and activities are built around the theme, and how students, faculty, staff, and alumni are engaged in the theme throughout the semester. The most notable outcome of the program has been the outpouring of support for the themed semester by a variety of constituents, thereby confirming the value of the program to the entire campus community.

In Chapter Three, "Helping the International Student Understand the American University," Mary Chang describes a campus development of an intensive English program to assist non-native speakers with their English proficiency so that they may pursue an academic degree. Chang describes how students spend time in the intensive English classroom reading, writing, listening, and speaking English in an attempt to become more proficient and to be able to better understand and participate in a traditional American university classroom. Students enrolled in the program are also educated on the process for transitioning into regular university academic programs, which is the end goal for most in this setting. In addition to coursework in English, students attend sporting and cultural events, visit popular local attractions, and interact with students and community members in an effort to strengthen their understanding of American culture, values, and history—the real benefit for any individual seeking international travel.

In Chapter Four, "Partners in Student Success," authors Clayton Tatro and Brad Hodson discuss how Fort Scott Community College (FSCC) and Pittsburg State University (PSU) used new statewide admission standards to create opportunities for underachieving students wishing to receive a four-year degree. While other community colleges and universities bemoaned the new standards, FSCC and PSU embraced the change and identified ways to help students and boost enrollment numbers for both campuses. Students enroll as FSCC students, but take general education courses on the campus of PSU. In addition, these community college students have many of the same campus privileges that university students have, including the ability to live in the residence halls, eat in the dining halls, attend university events as PSU students, and obtain PSU parking permits. When they have raised their grade-point averages to the level that will allow them to achieve regular admission to the university, they transition seamlessly into the university's academic system, thereby increasing retention and the rate of success beyond that realized by other transfer students.

In Chapter Five, "Knowledge Sourcing in IT Support Services," Sue Workman describes how one university has utilized the limitless information technology knowledge of students, faculty, and staff and marshaled that knowledge to help other users solve their information technology (IT) problems. Known as "crowdsourcing," the program allows individuals to post their technology questions to a website that then broadcasts the query to an online community of knowledgeable users. The origin of crowdsourcing was the growing demand of user support services, also known as the "help desk." The university's IT department hired large numbers of students who required extensive training in a variety of areas. Turnover was high and the program was expensive. The solution, evolving from a simple group of files that could be searched at a robust online support center, allows the institution to keep pace with the demand and retain knowledge that had in the past disappeared whenever an employee left the center. Today, users of the system reply to the original posting offering their insight into the issue. Users rate the responses, thereby creating a hierarchy of experts whose postings are highly valued for their clarity and accuracy by all users of the crowdsourcing system.

In Chapter Six, "The Student Success Coach," authors Claudia Neuhauser and Kendra Weber explore how a university created a supportive environment for meeting students' learning and developmental needs. The program combines academic advising, career exploration, professional development, and support services into a single program that gives students the opportunity to focus on the services they need to be successful. The effective student success coach interacts regularly with the faculty and the student without replacing the necessary interaction between those two parties. Coaches and faculty consult one another to identify students who are struggling and develop strategies for getting the students back on track. Neuhauser and Weber describe how the program has helped to implement Chickering and Gamson's best practices for prompt feedback to students and strengthened the institution's response time for students in need of intervention, all the while communicating high expectations for the students. This integrated approach to student engagement allows the success coach to interact with the student on multiple issues (academic advising, career planning, internships, study abroad, etc.) and offer an individualized service not available in traditionally de-centralized programs on many university campuses.

In Chapter Seven, "A Proactive Approach to Serving Military and Veteran Students," authors Tracey Moon and Geraldine Schma present solutions to issues that are unique to military and veteran students, such as handling the interruption caused by midsemester deployments, facilitating transcript evaluation, identifying and accessing financial benefits for veterans, and helping military students integrate into the classroom. The complexity and seriousness of issues facing veteran students returning to campus or enrolling for the first time is unparalleled in modern higher education. Moon and Schma describe a system of care where the veteran students are listened to and where a culture of "everybody plays" is supported. The "everybody plays" concept centers on engaging the entire university community in the care and success of veteran students. Faculty, administrators, as well as professionals in student affairs areas such as counseling, health services, and advising came together to create an environment that welcomed students with a military background and created unique programs to address their particular needs and situation. Students themselves had a great deal of input into the development of this program and the campus has been recognized by several veterans organizations for its entrepreneurial approach to assisting these men and women as they re-enter society and higher education following military service.

In Chapter Eight, "A Collaborative Approach to College and University Student Health and Wellness," Darren Fullerton addresses a new trend in combining university health centers and campus recreation centers to achieve synergy in a single facility. Rather than having health services and recreational programs competing for staff, finances, and facilities, Fullerton describes a scenario where these two program areas share a facility and integrate programming to better serve the needs of students. While campus recreation centers are viewed as assisting recruitment and retention of students and health centers with treating illness and injury, common programmatic offerings can be addressed collaboratively. Fullerton cites the opportunity to work together on lifestyle management: addressing weight, blood pressure, heart rate, flexibility, and body strength. Both campus recreation and health services have an interest in lifestyle management and can work together to create a program that provides students with a holistic approach to this area. Housing these two areas in the same facility enhances collaboration, efficiency of services, and interdepartmental communication between recreation and health services.

## Conclusion

A full exploration of all the issues facing student affairs professionals today would be nearly impossible. Instead, we have tried to give the reader a broad look at some of the timeliest and most important issues facing presidents, academic deans, student affairs professionals, and institutions today. Our hope is that this volume will encourage university leaders to take an entrepreneurial approach to addressing these issues on their own campus. The solutions to the issues described in this volume will not be entirely applicable to all colleges and universities. However, perhaps some kernel of information provided by the authors will spark an idea of how to address a similar issue on another campus, thereby increasing the effectiveness of student affairs programs nationwide and adding to the body of knowledge in this important area of institutional operations.

J. Bradford Hodson
Bruce W. Speck
Editors

*J. BRADFORD HODSON is the Vice President for University Advancement at Pittsburg State University in Kansas.*

*BRUCE W. SPECK is the President of Missouri Southern State University in Joplin.*

NEW DIRECTIONS FOR HIGHER EDUCATION • DOI: 10.1002/he

# 1

*A Course Concierge service helps students navigate a path through full classes and scheduling conflicts.*

# The Course Concierge Service

*Paul A. Neill*

The primary objective of the concierge service at the University of Nevada, Reno is to keep students on track to graduate in four years. The Concierge is charged with helping students enroll in the classes they need, not necessarily want, to graduate. This one charge defines the operational criteria. The service is available to all students, freshmen through seniors. It embraces new, continuing, returning, and transfer students. The service is not intended to help students reorganize a schedule that already includes the classes they need. Again, our task is to help students continue to progress to graduation rather than create the perfect schedule.

In an environment of decreasing state budgets and the consequent impact on higher education funding, students are facing increasing scheduling challenges. Growing enrollment and a commitment to reducing time-to-degree exacerbate the situation. Despite these constraints, our institution has made a commitment to students that they will have access to the classes they need to graduate, or to make reasonable progress towards graduation. To meet this commitment the university established the Course Concierge service. The service is housed in the office of the executive vice-president and provost.

## Accountability and the Metrics for Success

The Course Concierge service can be traced to the summer of 2007 when the academic leadership of the University of Nevada, Reno discussed and adopted a number of data metrics. These conversations took place in an environment of national discourse on increased accountability, and in a state where high school graduation and college going rates are among the lowest in the nation.

New Directions for Higher Education, no. 153, Spring 2011 © Wiley Periodicals, Inc.
Published online in Wiley Online Library (wileyonlinelibrary.com) • DOI: 10.1002/he.420

The first metric adopted was the number of enrolled undergraduate and graduate students. The university set a goal of increasing headcount by 500 each year for the next five years, through 2012, reaching a total student body of approximately 20,000 strong. Another metric targeted time-to-degree and identified a goal of increasing the six-year graduation rate by 12 percent in five years. Goals were also set to increase first-year persistence to 85 percent and second-year retention to 90 percent.

Teams worked to design and refine freshman recruiting, retention, and persistence strategies. They concluded that increasing student numbers may create unacceptable enrollment challenges for students, believing that targeted enrollment increases would be an obstacle to recruiting more freshmen and retaining them beyond the first year. Clearly, if we were successful in recruiting more students we must have adequate capacity in the freshman classes. To address this concern the president guaranteed that all freshmen would be enrolled in the classes they needed. To back up this guarantee, he enlisted the assistance of the director of the Core Curriculum. The Core Curriculum is the general education program at the university. Specifically, the director was to ensure that all freshmen could enroll in English and mathematics courses consistent with their standardized test or placement scores. This initial charge established the foundation for the Course Concierge service.

## Concierge Service Evolution

The university website promoted the concierge service. *Nevada News*, an online university newspaper, published articles describing the service, defining the target populations, and providing contact information for the Concierge office. Prior to the establishment of the concierge service, the director of the Core Curriculum worked closely with the freshman writing and math programs during registration periods to help them monitor enrollment supply and demand in the freshman classes. The Core office had an effective working relationship with these programs. This working knowledge of the freshman classes and the established relationship with programs across the campus was an excellent foundation on which to build the Course Concierge service. Therefore, we were immediately able to work proactively with the freshman population. As one might expect, we had already identified high demand in the core writing and math courses, and in the core social science and fine arts curricula. We consulted with the programs and each one developed contingency plans to accommodate the anticipated growth in the freshman class. The Concierge office provided enrollment projections based on recruitment data, and when necessary, advocated on behalf of the programs for resources to support additional class sections. We have now worked successfully through five registration periods.

In addition to growth in the freshman class, the academic leadership embraced the philosophy of increasing the number of students graduating in four years. The president has promoted what he refers to as a "culture of completion." Freshman orientation promotes the idea of "the freshman class," and the expectation that the "class" will graduate in four years. In addition, all undergraduate degree programs publish four-year recommended class schedules. However, before the establishment of the concierge service, anecdotal information suggested that curricular obstacles stood in the way of students attempting to graduate in four years. One such anecdote was centered on another component of the Core Curriculum, the senior capstone courses. These courses are writing-intensive and enrollments are limited to 35 students. The limited enrollments facilitate the inclusion of significant writing assignments in the classes. Anecdotes suggested that limited capacity in the capstone courses delayed graduation for a significant number of students. This and other similar concerns led the president to introduce the concierge service to assist all students with seemingly insurmountable enrollment challenges.

As the campus learned about the concierge service, students began to contact the Concierge office in increasing numbers. During each enrollment period, the concierge service assists over seventy students: more than half are juniors or seniors. Although it is more difficult to anticipate their enrollment challenges, we can identify patterns of need. Of particular note are high-demand courses in two specific areas: a major required upper-division College of Business courses, including capstones, and a select number of prerequisite science courses for biological science and health profession majors. We quickly developed lines of communication with the College of Business and departments in the natural sciences.

At the same time that the university introduced the concierge service, the College of Business developed an online application allowing business majors to request access to full courses. Once the students have self-identified, the college advisors and the Concierge office perform a degree audit to confirm that the student needs the course that particular semester to graduate or to make reasonable progress towards graduation. Once this is established, we contact the faculty member to advocate on behalf of the student, and secure permission to enroll the student in the class. The goal of this communication is to ensure that students who need access to the courses have priority. A primary service to faculty provided by the concierge service is that we can validate the student's need for enrollment. To date, we have received full cooperation from faculty in facilitating the students.

In contrast to the College of Business, capacity in the lower-division natural-science courses is at a premium. Infrastructure and graduate teaching assistant funding place constraints on the number of openings available in the laboratory sections. Student demand for the general chemistry classes and the anatomy and physiology sequence in biology is pushing the capacity limits in these classes. To accommodate student demand, the chemistry and biology departments have added summer sections. In addition, the opening of the Math and Science Center this year, and the Medical Education Building next year, provides much needed laboratory space.

NEW DIRECTIONS FOR HIGHER EDUCATION • DOI: 10.1002/he

## Course Concierge Service Criteria

Advisors across campus deal routinely with the many and varied enrollment challenges faced by our students. The services provided by the Course Concierge are not in competition with the excellent work done by our faculty and professional advisors. On the contrary, the concierge service should complement what they do. Indeed, the Concierge should be a resource supporting the work of the advisors. Every semester, advisors serve the needs of large numbers of students. We encourage them to refer the more complex and intractable enrollment challenges to the Course Concierge.

The concierge service is not designed to solve every enrollment challenge. Occasionally, students will ask for help to move from one class section to a full section simply for scheduling convenience. In these cases, we advise students to continue monitoring enrollment because it is not static. Often a seat will become available. For other students, course capacity is not the only obstacle. We check to confirm that the student has the required prerequisite course. Finally, if the student is a major in the program offering the course we ask the student to first exhaust all possibilities with the department advisor. We have found that almost without exception, our faculty, advisors, and departments will do everything possible, within the bounds of academic integrity, to help students stay on track.

Transfer students have begun to use the concierge service recently. This population has some unique constraints. The average transfer student on our campus transfers more than 50 credits of previous coursework. A significant number of these credits do not satisfy general education or major requirements. Thus, transfer students end up with more elective credits than needed to complete the degree. Therefore, it is critical that they enroll only in required credits. If, for one reason or another, the student needs to be enrolled as a full-time student he or she will have little or no flexibility in course selection. They must have access to the classes they need to stay on track. These students are a high priority.

## The Economy and Budget Reduction: The Perfect Storm

When the university established the concierge service no one could have predicted the full extent of the recent global economic downturn. As has been the case with many systems of public higher education, the Nevada System of Higher Education has suffered significant budget reductions. Over the 2010 and 2011 fiscal years, the university will have absorbed a 15.6% total budget reduction. The university chose to make strategic, rather than across-the-board, cuts. For example, the academic units' budgets have been reduced by an average of 9.1%, less than half the percentage reduction of the administrative units. However, 9.1% is a significant reduction and we now hire fewer temporary instructors. In lieu of a 4.6% salary reduction, tenured professors agreed to increase their student full-time equivalent production. In most cases faculty are teaching more students, but they are not teaching more sections. Student credit hours have not dropped. However, as a direct consequence of the budget reductions students are faced with fewer class sections and, therefore, reduced scheduling flexibility. We believe that the concierge service provides the additional support students need to negotiate this slightly less flexible environment.

## Advantages of a Centrally Located Concierge Service

The location of the Concierge in the office of the executive vice-president and provost has advantages for campus, faculty, and students. The primary advantage of this location to the campus is the flow of information through the office. The concierge service has helped us to identify several curricular constraints on student progress, including outdated and inaccurate information in the university general catalog, and unanticipated scheduling conflicts in recommended schedules. We also believe that the service generates goodwill both on- and off-campus. When we approach faculty advocating for a student, the faculty member can have confidence that the student truly needs to take the class. Of course, we believe that students benefit most from the service. We are full-service and if we cannot assist the student directly, we can always direct him or her to the faculty member or department representative who can.

## Conclusion

Not all students need the services of a Course Concierge. However, this service provides an effective and efficient enrollment management resource for the freshman class. In addition, the Concierge provides essential support for faculty and professional advisors struggling to find the time and resources to help students deal with the more challenging scheduling conflicts and find access to chronically full classes.

PAUL A. NEILL, *in addition to research and teaching at the University of Nevada, Reno, has served as Faculty Senate Chair. He now adjudicates a variety of student academic affairs issues on behalf of the provost, and serves as Course Concierge and the Director of the Core Curriculum and General Studies programs.*

NEW DIRECTIONS FOR HIGHER EDUCATION • DOI: 10.1002/he

**2**

*A regional university selects a different country to emphasize each fall semester to provide every student with a global experience.*

# Rendezvous with the World: Missouri Southern State University's Themed Semesters

*Chad Stebbins*

Missouri Southern State University (MSSU) is a state-supported, comprehensive university offering programs leading to the bachelor's degree and to selective master's degrees in collaboration with other universities. In 1995, Missouri Governor Mel Carnahan signed into law House Bill No. 442, which directed that MSSU "develop academic support programs and activities necessary to establish international or global education as the theme of its mission." That legislation was enacted as part of Missouri's "Blueprint for Higher Education," which provided every state university with a "mission enhancement." Missouri State University, for example, chose a mission in public affairs. The University of Central Missouri selected a mission in professional applied science and technology while Southeast Missouri State University focused on experiential learning. The universities all received additional funding from the legislature to implement their statewide missions.

MSSU faculty and administration designed a comprehensive plan of international education that included the establishment of the Institute of International Studies, charged with overseeing the internationalizing of the campus. The plan also established the following goals:

- To infuse the curriculum with a global perspective.
- To expand the learning of foreign languages.
- To provide Missouri Southern students with opportunities to gain an understanding of other cultures and international issues through study-abroad programs.
- To increase the participation of international students in campus activities.
- To create new majors in International Studies and International Business.

NEW DIRECTIONS FOR HIGHER EDUCATION, no. 153, Spring 2011 © Wiley Periodicals, Inc.
Published online in Wiley Online Library (wileyonlinelibrary.com) • DOI: 10.1002/he.421

As a result, MSSU has added well over 125 international courses to its catalog since the establishment of the "international mission" 15 years ago. Although enabling students to travel abroad is a thrust of the internationalization efforts, one-third of MSSU's 5,800 enrollment is comprised of nontraditional students who have obligations that preclude them from participating in conventional study-abroad programs. The MSSU student low-income rate of 58 percent—double the rate for the Missouri (28 percent) and US (29 percent) populations in general—also prohibits many from affording the experience. The unique concept of focusing a semester on an international theme was devised as a way to bring the world to every student at the university.

Each fall, a country or area of the world becomes the focal point for special courses and activities throughout the semester. Since 1997, MSSU has organized themed semesters focusing on China, Africa, Latin America, America, Japan, India, Cuba, Russia, Mexico, France, Germany, Canada, and Brazil. The semesters have expanded from around a dozen scheduled events to more than 65 on occasion. This innovative approach introduces students to at least four different cultures during a typical undergraduate education. Faculty with expertise in the highlighted country work to develop special course offerings for the semester. Extracurricular lectures, concerts, films, and other activities are arranged by the Institute of International Studies. All faculty members are encouraged to incorporate the country of emphasis into their classrooms as much as possible.

Themed semesters serve to internationalize the campus and community in terms of fostering an understanding of how cultures and societies around the world evolve and are sustained. It is a goal of MSSU that graduates will have empathy for the values and perspectives of cultures other than their own and an awareness of international and multicultural influences in their own lives. In many ways, themed semesters have succeeded in broadening the university's outlook beyond a traditional internal focus and have engendered in the faculty, student body, and community an understanding of how they are affected by global events.

The country selected every year must be vital to the United States and an important player on the world stage. For example, MSSU is unlikely to announce a Malta Semester, a Liechtenstein Semester, or even an Australia Semester. Indeed, the university has chosen all four BRIC countries (Brazil, Russia, India, and China) this decade with the belief that if popular theory holds, these four nations would become the world's most dominant economies by 2050. A faculty committee makes the selections, often three or four years in advance. One practical consideration is whether we can find enough cultural events—touring performing groups, films, and art exhibits—to build a complete repertoire of events. For that reason, an Afghanistan Semester or an Iraqi Semester is highly improbable.

China has been the only country selected twice, in 1997 and 2007. The focus the first time was on Hong Kong's transfer of sovereignty from the

United Kingdom to the People's Republic of China. The second China Semester featured 39 events and total attendance of 8,790—the first time we tracked both on-campus and community participation. Twice we have selected a continent (Africa in 1998) or region of the world (Latin America in 1999) with the opinion that it would be problematic to select one country to represent those areas. But faculty now seem to prefer that a single country always be chosen. When the director of the Institute of International Studies proposed that MSSU emphasize either the entire Middle East or the Arab World for fall 2011, the faculty instead voted for Egypt to represent that part of the globe. A proposal from the head of the English department for a Scandinavia Semester also was rejected, and the faculty didn't think that Sweden, Norway, Denmark, Finland, or Iceland were sufficient countries to stand on their own. Instead, Thailand (2012), Italy (2013), and Turkey (2014) were chosen.

## Building a Slate of Activities

An ad hoc committee of faculty members and an occasional student or two begins meeting in January to plan the activities for the upcoming fall semester. Some faculty are on the committee every year; others serve only when the upcoming country holds a particular interest. The themed semester's average budget of $30,000 is spent on honoraria and travel expenses for guest speakers, performing groups on tour in the United States, public performance rights for films, banners, brochures, and advertising. MSSU invites faculty experts from the University of Missouri, the University of Kansas, the University of Arkansas, and Missouri State University and offers them honoraria of $500 or $600 plus mileage for giving two or three presentations. Occasionally, an expert is brought in from outside the region, such as in fall 2008 when the Germany Semester committee wanted a program on the German Autobahn and the only authority in the United States was a professor of history at the University of Maryland.

One of the highlights of the Fall 2009 Canada Semester was the appearance of a "Mountie"—a member of the Royal Canadian Mounted Police (RCMP). It was no small task, though, getting bureaucratic approval and then finding a Mountie willing to come all the way to Joplin, Missouri. When a visit to the RCMP website did not provide any information about a speakers' bureau, the director of the Institute of International Studies contacted a professor of criminal justice at the University of Central Missouri (UCM), which had sponsored a Canadian Justice Conference on its campus in 2006. One of the speakers at the UCM conference was a staff sergeant with the RCMP who subsequently turned down MSSU's invitation to speak as he had recently retired. However, he did put the university in touch with the superintendent in charge of the Nanaimo, British Columbia, Detachment, who in turn passed on the request to the RCMP division office in Vancouver. Three months later, after numerous emails, phone calls, and faxes to the RCMP, MSSU finally had its man. Inspector A. F. O'Donnell, a thirty-five-year veteran of the force, gave three presentations to criminal justice majors and other interested students, toured the university's criminal justice department, and received coverage from the local daily newspaper during a whirlwind twenty-four-hour visit.

A recent trend has been to utilize MSSU faculty with expertise in the country as featured speakers. Eight faculty teamed up early in the Canada Semester for a three-hour program on what Canada has in common with the United States and how it is also uniquely different. The topics included "The Mouse That Roars: Canada and U.S. Economic Relations," "The Rowdy Upstairs Neighbors: The Canadian Geographic Mosaic," and "Hot It's Not But It Rocks a Lot." Later in the semester, a professor of English gave a presentation on Canadian pianist Glenn Gould, who stunned both his fans and critics by retiring from the concert stage at the height of his career. The Brazil Semester included talks by the head of the theatre department on the Christ the Redeemer statue—one of the new Seven Wonders of the World—and an assistant professor of teacher education on the "marvelous city" of Rio de Janeiro. Though the presentations by MSSU faculty do not result in the same level of excitement for the campus community as bringing in an "expert" from a prestigious university, they hold one distinct advantage—they're free!

The Gockel International Symposium, held every September or October, is the centerpiece of the themed semester. Funded by an endowment created by a longtime faculty member, the one- or two-day symposium has brought in such renowned speakers as Senator Paul Simon, Nobel Peace Prize winner Oscar Arias, Richard Haass (president of the Council on Foreign Relations), Nina Khrushcheva (granddaughter of the former Soviet Premier), and *New York Times* best-selling author David Grann.

Despite the heavy emphasis on meaty topics and intellectual stimulation, the most popular aspect of the themed semesters remains the concerts. At least one major performance is scheduled every year, often a great undertaking by the Institute of International Studies and the technicians in the Taylor Performing Arts Center. The Canada Semester featured Great Big Sea, a platinum-selling, folk-rock band from Newfoundland that even has a large following in the United States. MSSU was able to secure Great Big Sea for a heavily discounted fee of $8,000, as the band had an open date on its calendar as it headed toward a performance in Louisville, Kentucky. (The Consulate General of Canada–Chicago Office chipped in $3,500 toward the cost.) The concert drew an estimated audience of 1,000 and brought Great Big Sea fans to the campus from as far away as Oklahoma City and Tulsa, Oklahoma.

### The Themed Semester and the First-Year Experience Program: A Perfect Match

The most significant outcome of the themed semester approach to global education at MSSU has been the widespread participation of the entire university.

New Directions for Higher Education • DOI: 10.1002/he

The most visible has been the First-Year Experience Program (FYE), created in 2007 to assist first-year students in the transition to university life and to introduce them to the academic and international opportunities at the university. Under the auspices of the FYE Program, MSSU also replaced its one-hour freshman orientation course with a new three-hour course titled "The University Experience: Transitions within an International Context." The University Experience is a required fundamentals course designed to assist first-year students in successfully defining themselves both as active participants in the MSSU community and as citizens of a twenty-first-century global community. The course emphasizes participation in MSSU's international mission; students study the themed semester country, attend international events, and are introduced to international programs and study-abroad opportunities offered by the university.

The instructors require their students to attend three to five themed semester activities, and most offer extra credit for going to additional events. "They had to include how what they heard at the events might affect them as a college student and/or global citizen in the reflection papers they were required to write," said Nancy Schiavone, a reference librarian who taught the University Experience course in fall 2009. "They were often asked and had to answer questions on tests and quizzes about how anything that we learned during the course of the semester related to them as first-year university students, how it might connect them to a globalized world, and how it could affect them as global citizens of the future."

Josie Mai, an assistant professor of art, divided her fall 2009 class into small groups and required each group to build a freestanding, three-dimensional totem pole in celebration of the Canada Semester. The totem poles had to be at least three feet tall and represent the group's collective and individual identities. Students also prepared PowerPoint presentations on Emily Carr, the Canadian artist and writer who often painted native totem poles in the coastal villages of British Columbia.

Stephanie Goad, the international student advisor, devised an activity called "Meet the Canadians" where her class held a question-and-answer session live on Skype video with a recent Canadian graduate of MSSU now attending law school in Saskatchewan and a current MSSU student from Manitoba. "We incorporated many aspects of Canada, from education and sports to the political system, to famous Canadians, to international trade between the United States and Canada," Goad said. "The students said it was a very interesting way to learn about Canada and internationalization."

## The MSSU Common Reading Program

For each themed semester, a related book is chosen as a common reading for use in all sections of The University Experience course. Students read, discuss, and study the book, as well as its author. The book is chosen by committee prior to the start of the academic year. A speaker related to the reading (i.e., author, translator, character) comes to campus to lecture and meet with the first-year students and the campus as a whole.

Klee Wyck, a collection of literary sketches by Emily Carr, was the common reader for the Canada Semester. Kathryn Bridge, the editor of the 2003 version of Klee Wyck, spent two days on campus in November 2009 discussing the Canadian classic as well as Carr, regarded as one of the country's national treasures. Carr died in 1945, but Bridge brought the eccentric artist and author to life for the hundreds of students and faculty who attended her three presentations and two classroom visits. MSSU's Literary Lions Book Club, consisting of twenty-five community members and a faculty moderator, also read Klee Wyck during the Canada Semester.

For the Germany Semester, the common reader was After the Wall: Confessions of an East German Childhood and the Life That Came Next by Jana Hensel. In the book, Jana Hensel recounts her childhood growing up in the German Democratic Republic and the changes that took place after the Berlin Wall fell when she was thirteen years old. Hensel came to MSSU for three days in October 2008 to read and discuss excerpts from her book, meet with faculty and student peer mentors teaching The University Experience course, visit individual classes, and conduct book signings. More than 1,000 students and faculty attended her three public presentations.

## Participation by Other Departments

Beginning with the Fall 2002 India Semester, Southern Theatre has presented a play from the themed country every year. In 2009, the department staged the US premiere of Canadian playwright Herman Voaden's Emily Carr. The production tied in nicely with Klee Wyck, Carr's literary sketches. "Our participation in the themed semesters serves a number of worthy purposes: our actors, designers, and directors have the opportunity to work with material from other countries and other theatrical traditions that moves us beyond our standard repertoire," said Dr. James Lile, director of Southern Theatre. "The theatrical production augments the guest lectures and musical events by providing the students with another channel through which to experience the featured country."

Behind the Southern Symphony Orchestra, which has presented an annual concert of music from the themed country for the past five years, the music department also has been a major contributor to the program. Finding Canadian orchestral music was a particular challenge for the symphony's director, who ultimately discovered that Canada has produced a surprisingly rich repertoire. The MSSU Symphonic Band and Wind Ensemble presented a winter concert, "Celebrating Canada and Christmas," to end the Canada Semester. For the Fall 2010 Brazil Semester, a professor of music organized the Bossa Nova Jazz Collective, a jazz sextet consisting of professional musicians from Southwest Missouri. Tying in with the Brazilian theme, the President's Third Annual Gala Concert, "A Night in the Tropics," featured such classics as "One Note Samba," "Aquarela do Brasil," and the MSSU president himself singing "The Girl from Ipanema."

KXMS, the university's classical music radio station, plays not only the national anthems of each themed country but also myriad hours of music from the country. In preparation for the Canada Semester, KXMS put out a call for recordings produced in the True North, with the result that Analekta Records, a French Canadian import label, provided a number of recordings. French Canadian violinist Angele Dubeau, represented on several Analekta releases, was interviewed by KXMS general manager Jeff Skibbe. For the Brazil Semester, KXMS aired Brazilian music and Brazilian performers; Heitor Villa Lobos, one of the most notable Brazilian composers, aired on "Southern Serenade"; and Brazilian cellist Antonio Meneses was featured in a premiere recording of "Cello Concertino" by Brazil-born Clóvis Pereira dos Santos.

An assistant professor of art with expertise in drawing and printmaking has designed the official logo and T-shirt of the themed semester for the past three years. The art department also secures an exhibition of original prints every year for a four-week display in its Spiva Art Gallery to open the semester.

The Robert W. Plaster School of Business Administration hosted an academic and business conference as part of the 2007 China Semester that focused on the linkages between the country's historical, social, and cultural past and its current business practices. Titled "The Dragon Awake: China & Its Emergence as a Global Business Leader," the two-day conference was funded in part by a US Department of Education Title VI-B grant.

The English Department coordinated a series of readings by faculty and students for both the Canada and Brazil Semesters. The Canada readings focused on native and Aboriginal writers, national Canadian literature, and francophone Canadian literature; the Brazil readings focused on nineteenth-century literature, early twentieth-century-literature, and later twentieth-century literature.

The Film Society at Missouri Southern, founded in 1962, has shown films from the country of emphasis for the last seven fall semesters. The Society's continuing offering of films from other countries are shown in the spring semesters. Director Harrison Kash credits the themed semester for doubling the attendance at his films. He was stunned to see sixty-five people show up to see the silent 1922 classic "Nanook of the North" during the Canada Semester.

Athletics recently became involved in the themed semesters when the Athletic Director provided prime space outside the football stadium for two mini-Oktoberfests during the Germany Semester. Both Oktoberfests featured German brass bands playing before and after the football games. One of the bands, from Kansas City, even marched in the MSSU homecoming parade before the game.

The library and registrar's office have contributed by creating displays promoting the themed semester. The Literary Lions Book Club typically reads a book from or about the country; in fall 2010, participants were enthralled by David Grann's *The Lost City of Z: A Tale of Deadly Obsession in the Amazon*. A professor of biology who maintains a botanical bulletin board in her building always includes the flora of the featured country as well as the products and crops that originated there. KGCS, the university-owned television station, tapes several of the lectures and concerts and rebroadcasts them on two area cable systems. Sodexho, the campus food service provider, prepared a special Brazilian dinner in the cafeteria one evening. That the themed semester has permeated the fabric of the institution is without question.

## Conclusion

Although most universities emphasize study abroad as the primary vehicle to internationalize the campus, in reality only a small percentage of students actually participate in this endeavor. The internationally themed semesters at Missouri Southern State University reach virtually every student, and provide a global perspective and cultural enrichment for the university's external communities.

*CHAD STEBBINS is Director of the Institute of International Studies and a professor of Communication at Missouri Southern State University in Joplin.*

New Directions for Higher Education • DOI: 10.1002/he

# 3

*Intensive English programs provide many opportunities for international students to connect with American students and other international students, as well as to feel part of a global community.*

# Helping the International Student Understand the American University

*Mary Chang*

To be successful in navigating the waters of American higher education, international students need to demonstrate proficiency in the English language and an understanding of the educational expectations of American academia.

Unlike Americans who apply to a US university, international students must demonstrate that they understand enough English to take a class at a university without much difficulty. Many universities require a language proficiency examination such as the Test of English as a Foreign Language (TOEFL™). Although preparing for such a test can be done in the student's home country, many international students choose to prepare by attending an English as a Second Language (ESL) program in the United States prior to gaining admittance into an American undergraduate or graduate program. By doing this, international students have the chance of improving their level of English while experiencing American life.

The American English and Culture Program (AECP) is an intensive ESL program based at the Tempe campus of Arizona State University (ASU). AECP is a non-degree, non-credit program that prepares international students to meet the language requirement for acceptance into ASU or other American universities. AECP runs five eight-week sessions a year with six levels of English proficiency: Basic 1, Basic 2, Intermediate 1, Intermediate 2, Advanced 1, and Advanced 2. The classes offered to students enrolled in AECP include the combined skills of reading/writing and listening/speaking, as well as a range of electives in areas such as grammar, vocabulary, pronunciation, communication, and business English.

New students to AECP are given an exam that determines their initial placement level in the program. After being placed in the program, if a student successfully masters all of the objectives for a specific level, that student

New Directions for Higher Education, no. 153, Spring 2011 © Wiley Periodicals, Inc.
Published online in Wiley Online Library (wileyonlinelibrary.com) • DOI: 10.1002/he.422

21

will enter the next level in the following session. A majority of our students are able to complete the program in eighteen months or less depending on their initial placement level. Through an agreement between AECP and ASU, students who complete Advanced 2 with grades of B or better can be admitted into an undergraduate or graduate program at ASU in lieu of a TOEFL™ score. This means that the quality of the courses offered in AECP, especially at the Advanced 2 level, must be equal to what is considered to be a successful entrance score on the TOEFL™.

In addition to the regular (the standard eight-week) program, AECP also offers several special programs that are tailored to the needs of a specific population. For example, we have arranged four-week teacher-training programs for teacher groups from South Korea, the People's Republic of China, and the French Ministry of Education. Because these participants have limited time and they do not intend to enter an American university, AECP provides them with a special curriculum that offers more English language training, exposure to the latest teaching methodologies/approaches, and exposure to American culture.

## Opening the Window to Studies in America

Over the course of a year, AECP enrolls 800 to 1,000 students from over sixty different nations. For the majority of students, success in the university classroom is the goal. To meet that goal, AECP students attend weekly reading/writing and listening/speaking classes for twenty-one hours and a three-hour elective course. As students gain more experience and a greater understanding of English, teachers encourage students to go beyond the classroom to build on their abilities.

For instance, a few of the advanced-level teachers have their students observe a class that would be a requirement for his or her intended major and then write a report, noting the difficulty of the subject and the level of English needed to participate in the class. As non-native English speakers, students find that this observation of a future required course is a revelation. They usually study harder because they now know how wide the gap is between their English level and what is required in a typical college class.

Students are encouraged to attend the AECP Reading Theater, a weekly activity open to all active AECP students regardless of level. Students engage in silent reading, group reading, or reading aloud individually a modified reader (a short story or novel that has been adjusted for the ESL student), while the Reading Theater teacher asks the students to pause to highlight vocabulary, idioms, and cultural usage of expressions. Students then get to view the movie version of the story, which allows them to hear the tone, rhythm, and intonations of English, and relate the words to the story's action and interactions between characters.

As the Reading Theater provides opportunities for students to build on their reading skills, the Conversation Club and Conversation Partner program

New Directions for Higher Education • DOI: 10.1002/he

help students to build on their speaking skills. The Conversation Club and Conversation Partner program are open to students in AECP and ASU. The Conversation Club is held weekly at a café on campus, and ASU students who are interested in traveling to or are currently studying about another country can often find a local expert among our AECP students. Sometimes topics are offered to get conversations started, but often this is not necessary. The Conversation Partner program is where AECP students who wish to have more opportunities to practice English are matched with ASU students studying a foreign language. Partners then develop a schedule for getting together and determine how much of the scheduled time is devoted to each language. Several partners have developed friendships that last well after AECP students have completed their ESL studies.

## New Offerings for Changing Times

As AECP has grown over the past five years, some topics or questions have arisen so often that special workshops have been developed to address them. For example, because successfully completing AECP is for many international students the last step before gaining admittance into ASU, it was important that ACEP students have information about the steps needed to facilitate admission. Therefore, representatives from ASU's Undergraduate and Graduate Admissions offices often conducted a number of the workshops, which focused primarily on the necessary documentation and deadlines. Many students have been spared extended delays in being admitted to ASU because the workshops identified critical parts of the application process that had to be completed. Other workshops focus on campus jobs and US culture, and some offer college/discipline-specific advisement.

Recently there has been a shift in the program to reflect newly enrolled students' interests in English as used in the sciences and away from academic and business-based English. New content-based elective classes have been developed to prepare these students for their future studies. Some of the new electives include Technical Writing and Research Methods; English for Science and Technology; English for Sustainability: Environment, Economics, and Equity; Food Matters: American Cooking, Nutrition, and Sustainability; as well as Building Matter: American Architecture and Design. Students' response to these new courses has been positive and there is growing enrollment.

## Experiencing American Culture

One key reason to study abroad is to experience a culture directly. Some students make homestay arrangements so they can experience American culture in a family setting. As an intensive ESL program, we try to provide as many opportunities to learn about American culture as possible in the eight weeks students attend a session. These activities help students explore culture on the ASU campus, the culture of the Tempe area and surrounding cities, and the culture of Arizona. For example, students carve pumpkins for Halloween, eat a Thanksgiving meal, and enjoy a small town parade in old-time Prescott for the Fourth of July, just to name a few.

Several resources are available to all ASU students, including those from AECP. Recreation facilities like the Student Recreation Complex and Sparky's Den give students a place to be physically fit, enjoy sports, and play group-oriented games. For organized team sports, our students are encouraged to join the many established student sports clubs or create their own. These clubs help our students to interact socially with diverse people who share a common interest. We also provide for attendance at a university or professional sporting event such as an ASU football game, a Phoenix Suns' basketball game, or an Arizona Diamondbacks' baseball game. The rules of the game are presented beforehand, and AECP teachers and staff are available at the game to explain events as they are happening.

In addition to sporting events, AECP students visit museums, the zoo, and other popular sightseeing areas across the state. Originally, as part of the architectural sustainability elective only, we visited Taliesin West, which was designed and developed by Frank Lloyd Wright. However, because the activity was so popular, we now include it in the general program. We also provide field-based learning opportunities by having our students explore locations like Sedona and the Grand Canyon.

Instead of traveling to learn about Arizona, we sometimes have guest speakers give presentations to our students. Some of our most popular activities include demonstrations of Native American hoop dancing and interactive country dancing. The presenters explain the cultural significance and regional importance of these activities.

## Conclusion

Our students may not have had the chance to experience a number of educational and cultural opportunities had they not been incorporated into their studies. The American English and Culture Program provides the opportunity for international students to become fully prepared for academic study at the university level, while building on their experiences of American as well as global community, communication, connection, and cooperation.

*MARY CHANG is Associate Director of the American English and Culture Program at the Tempe campus of Arizona State University. She has been teaching English as a Second Language domestically and English as a Foreign Language overseas for more than twenty years.*

NEW DIRECTIONS FOR HIGHER EDUCATION • DOI: 10.1002/he

*Pittsburg State University and Fort Scott Community College built a bridge program to make education more accessible to students.*

# Partners in Student Success

*Clayton N. Tatro, J. Bradford Hodson*

When Kansas changed the admission requirements for resident high school students to attend one of the six public institutions in the state, Pittsburg State University (PSU) and Fort Scott Community College (FSCC) saw an opportunity. Although cooperative programs between four-year and two-year institutions in Kansas had been rare because of territorial disputes, these two institutions saw the need to create a bridge program for those students who did not meet the new admission criteria.

Rather than tell such students that they would have to drive over sixty miles round trip to the nearest community college, PSU invited FSCC to offer courses on its campus, increasing opportunities for local students and enrollment for both schools. The result was an entrepreneurial program that offers underprepared students the chance to take advantage of the educational opportunities offered by a quality two-year college and the cultural, recreational, and intellectual amenities offered by a four-year regional university. Such a program has produced far more than additional credit-hour production. It also has created a partnership that has had an economic impact on both communities.

## Institutional Profiles

FSCC, founded in 1919, is a public community college located in Fort Scott, Kansas, ninety miles south of Kansas City. Governed by a six-member board of trustees, the college operates under the rules and regulations of the Kansas Board of Regents (KBOR). In addition to a general education transfer curriculum, FSCC also offers a diverse array of occupational programs, including cosmetology; commercial truck driving; environmental technology; farm and ranch management; business; construction trades and masonry; nursing and allied health; criminal justice; Harley-Davidson motorcycle training; John Deere agricultural technology; and heating, ventilation, and air conditioning.

New Directions for Higher Education, no. 153, Spring 2011 © Wiley Periodicals, Inc.
Published online in Wiley Online Library (wileyonlinelibrary.com) • DOI: 10.1002/he.423

Founded in 1903, PSU is a four-year comprehensive public university located in Pittsburg, Kansas, 120 miles south of Kansas City. Although FSCC has its own governing board and has its programs coordinated by KBOR, PSU is directly governed by the KBOR. The KBOR system is comprised of seven public universities while simultaneously coordinating the programs for nineteen community colleges and six technical colleges. Pittsburg State offers over 100 undergraduate-degree programs and fifty graduate-degree programs in four academic colleges: arts and sciences, business, technology, and education. The university has an enrollment of 7,200 students, 95 percent of which take classes on the institution's main campus.

## Qualified Admission in Kansas

In 1996, the Kansas legislature passed a law that established qualified admission standards for the state's six public universities. The new statute allowed all Kansas high school graduates to gain admission to any of the six KBOR institutions by meeting one of three criteria: an ACT score of 21 or higher; rank in the top one-third of their high school class; or a 2.0 grade point average (GPA) or higher on a prescribed pre-college high school curriculum. Although other criteria were established for general education diploma (GED) graduates, students twenty-one or older, and transfer students, most individuals who participated in the qualified admission program (QAP) were traditional high school graduates. When this law became effective in August 2001, it signaled Kansas as the last state in the nation to adopt a selective or qualified admission standard. Since 1915, Kansas had operated under an open admission policy guaranteeing admission to anyone who graduated from an accredited high school in Kansas.

## The New Law's Impact on Pittsburg State University

The new admission requirements created concern at PSU, which had long enjoyed a close relationship with the city and the Southeast Kansas region. A large number of the university's students came from its namesake community and the surrounding small towns, and local support for the university was strong. The new legislative mandate raised concerns that dictating admission criteria might exclude the children and grandchildren of local citizens who took extraordinary pride in "their" university. University officials who had enthusiastically and publicly supported the open-door policy used by the university for over seventy-five years felt particular angst.

In the years leading up to the new qualified admission standards, officials at the state's six public universities felt pressure from the legislature and KBOR to refine and clarify their missions. For example, in the mid-1980s, KBOR issued a directive that the public universities were to stop offering many of their associate-degree programs. PSU, offering several programs at the associate-degree level, expressed concern about losing these offerings

NEW DIRECTIONS FOR HIGHER EDUCATION • DOI: 10.1002/he

and, subsequently, the stream of transfer students who often moved from the associate-degree program into baccalaureate programs at PSU.

PSU resolved its concerns about the loss of the associate-degree programs by bringing in a regional partner to meet the needs of the students in programs the university could no longer deliver—enter FSCC. FSCC was first asked to come into Crawford County, Kansas, home of PSU, in 1985 to take over PSU's cosmetology program after KBOR's mandate was enacted that associate-degree programs be removed from four-year university curriculums. In subsequent years, Pittsburg State would move several more of its associate-degree programs, such as its heating, ventilation, and air conditioning, to FSCC under the same KBOR mandate. Consequently, when Kansas passed the new qualified admission standards in 1996, PSU turned again to FSCC for help in addressing university and student concerns.

## Working Together to Meet Both Student and Institutional Needs

The partnership between FSCC and PSU that evolved after the creation of the new qualified admission standards in 1996 permits students who do not qualify for regular admission to Pittsburg State under the new standards to take general education courses on PSU's campus while being enrolled as a FSCC student. Known as the Shared Campus Program, not only does this effort address the academic needs of underprepared students, but it also has boosted the enrollment of both FSCC and PSU. This unique solution defied the conventional wisdom at the time. No university in Kansas had previously welcomed a community college to provide face-to-face instruction in its home county, let alone on campus. The community colleges in Kansas all have well-defined service areas to which their programs are restricted and are not allowed to offer courses in the home county of a public university without written permission from that university's president. Within the span of a few months, PSU and FSCC would reach a "handshake" agreement that allowed FSCC to offer general education courses for underprepared students on the PSU campus.

Dick Hedges, former president of FSCC, and Tom Bryant, former president of PSU, were largely responsible for the informal arrangement by which the QAP developed at both institutions. The two men were and are longtime friends, having competed and coached against each other on the high school athletic fields of Southeast Kansas. Both admit that their personal relationship with one another greatly contributed to their ability to come together in partnership to serve the needs of underprepared students. The mutual trust and respect they held for each other allowed them to overcome any institutional hostility that is often present when one entity comes into another's home territory. In fact, the pact most likely would not have proven successful had other players been involved. The comfort level between these colleagues made this unique partnership possible.

NEW DIRECTIONS FOR HIGHER EDUCATION • DOI: 10.1002/he

Embracing its mission as a regional university, PSU wanted to ensure that students from Southeast Kansas had access to a great education, regardless of their status within the new qualified admission standards. With these new restrictions on admission and pressure to move away from two-year programs, PSU was particularly sensitive to losing opportunities for students. For Bryant, that meant "getting outside of yourself and doing what is right for students" (Tom Bryant, personal communication, August 26, 2010). He espoused the notion that a regional university should not be teaching training programs that belonged at the associate-degree level. "To have quality and efficient programs, we can't be all things to all people," he stated. Knowing that increased access to the training programs offered by FSCC greatly enhanced the economic development of the region, he quipped, "How can anyone fault what we are trying to do?"

During interviews with both past presidents, remarkably similar, overarching themes quickly emerged. Hedges continually reinforced doing "what is good for students" (Dick Hedges, personal communication, August 24, 2010). Bryant's interview mantra reinforced the belief that the Shared Campus Program created by the two institutions was "the right thing to do to meet the students' needs" (Tom Bryant, personal communication, August 26, 2010). The result of these two leaders' quiet, confident resolve was an original, one-of-a-kind design that has remained strong and stable, steadily growing and developing over the last eleven years.

## The Shared Campus Agreement

Despite almost universal belief in the power of this partnership, Hedges and Bryant both acknowledged that legitimate concerns were present in the detail of the informal agreement. Supervisory staff at both institutions had real reservations as to the execution of the plan. If PSU was going to open its campus to another college, protections needed to be put in place to ensure that PSU students were not "poached" by Fort Scott and that PSU's enrollment was not cannibalized. Staff from both institutions insisted that the original "handshake" agreement between the two campus presidents evolve into a written agreement that clearly outlined guidelines and responsibilities for all parties involved. The result, a document titled "A Shared Campus Agreement," debuted in 1997 and delineated expectations and outcomes for both institutions and the students who participated in the QAP. The title of this memorandum of understanding reflects the mutual respect and reciprocity between PSU and FSCC.

Eligibility to participate in the Shared Campus Program at PSU and FSCC is limited to students who meet one of the following conditions:

- Students who do not meet qualified admission requirements for degree-seeking status at PSU.

- Current FSCC students.
- Students who are a permanent resident of Crawford County, Kansas.

Following the same requirements of PSU students, all first-year students participating in the Shared Campus Program must live in a university residence hall for their first two academic semesters on campus and purchase a meal plan. After their freshman year, students may live in housing of their choice, on-campus or off-campus. Exceptions to the policy exist, but are again consistent with current PSU policies. Shared Campus Program students eligible for financial aid sign a waiver with FSCC that allows them to transfer their financial aid funds to PSU to cover room and board expenses.

Shared Campus Program students are permitted to obtain a PSU student ID (a Gorilla Card) once they have enrolled and paperwork has been completed with PSU. The PSU Gorilla Card is needed to obtain the services offered through the campus privilege fees. In addition, with a PSU Gorilla Card, Shared Campus Program students may participate in PSU clubs and organizations, and have access to PSU athletic events, access to Student Activities Council events, and use of the Overman Student Center. Other services offered through the Shared Campus Program include access to services at the PSU student health and counseling center, university recreational facilities, and the opportunity to obtain a PSU parking permit. In addition, all books required for courses in the FSCC/PSU Shared Campus Program are available in the PSU bookstore. Though Shared Campus Program students are welcomed on the PSU campus, there are limitations. QAP students may not hold membership in PSU fraternities or sororities, PSU intercollegiate athletics, ROTC, or student government.

## Evaluating Success of the Shared Campus Program

To evaluate the success of the partnership with PSU through the Shared Campus Program, FSCC collects data on the number of students who are enrolled and the success rate of completers in the Shared Campus Program. From 2001–2009, 40.5 percent of students enrolled in the Shared Campus Program matriculated to PSU (104 of 257 students). Of those students, 54.8 percent have either graduated or are still enrolled (57 of 104 students.)

Each year, representatives from FSCC and PSU meet to discuss and evaluate the performance of the Shared Campus Program in crucial areas including housing, financial aid, and accounts payable/receivable. Both institutions have concluded that the Shared Campus Program has exceeded expectations. Consequently, the program has been modified and expanded to meet the educational needs of even more students. To date, the Shared Campus Program has been extended to FSCC's Harley-Davidson and John Deere technician programs.

NEW DIRECTIONS FOR HIGHER EDUCATION • DOI: 10.1002/he

## Benefits for Students

The benefits of the Shared Campus Program extend beyond what is gained for the two institutions. Students benefit as well. Individuals who begin their postsecondary academic careers as part of the FSCC/PSU on-campus partnership graduate at a higher rate than those who begin their work on the campus of another community or technical college and then transfer to PSU's campus. The sources of this academic success are multiple. First is the familiarity with Pittsburg State's campus. Having spent two years attending classes, using the library, interacting with PSU students and faculty members, and being, in general, a part of the PSU family, FSCC students feel an automatic affinity with the university upon transfer. As a FSCC student, these individuals have taken classes in and around the academic department that now houses their major, they have visited with or taken classes from PSU professors in their chosen field, and they have benefited from a curriculum during their time as a FSCC student that is coordinated and endorsed by PSU. This means that upon transfer, they begin their advanced studies in academic surroundings nearly identical to what they experienced as a FSCC student. Not only is this transition seamless from an academic perspective, but also from a student life perspective. Students do not need to obtain new parking passes, they continue to live in the same PSU residence halls if they wish, their meals are taken in the same place they have eaten for the last two years, and their afternoons and evenings are filled with familiar recreation and entertainment options. They use the same library, computer labs, student health and counseling services, and enrollment management processes they have for up to two years. For students, this level of comfort makes the transfer from community college student to university student not just seamless, but in some ways unnoticeable. This comfort contributes significantly to their success as a student pursuing a bachelor's degree from PSU.

## Benefits for Fort Scott Community College

The success of the Shared Campus Program has given FSCC a larger presence within the region and has led to additional partnership opportunities. With FSCC personnel on PSU's campus and additional partner programs added since the program began (Harley-Davidson, John Deere, HVAC, construction trades) FSCC operates several instructional sites in Pittsburg and Crawford County. This presence in a larger population center gives FSCC greater visibility and name recognition in a key market. Bourbon County, Kansas, home of FSCC, has 15,000 citizens; Crawford County, Kansas, by comparison, has over 38,000 residents. Greater name recognition in Crawford County will be of significant importance to FSCC in the future as this partnership with PSU develops.

Through the Shared Campus Program, FSCC generates nearly 3,000 credit hours per year and more than 8,000 in Crawford County at the invitation of PSU. These courses are often taught by PSU adjunct faculty, thereby giving FSCC access to a greater pool for adjunct faculty for their programs, both on the PSU campus and in other FSCC programs. These "shared" faculty help to maintain high academic standards of instructional quality at both PSU and Fort Scott.

## Benefits to Pittsburg State University

Just as FSCC benefits from the relationship it has with PSU, so too does PSU benefit from this ongoing joint operation. PSU sees many advantages to having a two-year college offer courses directly on its campus.

Transfer Students. Approximately two hundred FSCC students take classes on the PSU campus through the Shared Campus Program. For them it is an opportunity to stay close to home, pay a lower tuition rate, and feel a part of a larger university culture. For PSU, it is a consistent source of transfer students into the institution for bachelor's degrees. On average, 40 percent of the FSCC students continue their academic work at PSU in pursuit of a four-year degree. This represents a much higher transfer rate to Pittsburg State than from any of Kansas' other twenty-five community and technical colleges. Transfer students comprise approximately 9 percent of PSU's total enrollment. Therefore, continuing this stream of incoming junior-level students from the on-campus programs of FSCC is in the best interest of the university.

Economic Impact. A 2008 economic impact study conducted by PSU showed that each of the institution's 7,200 students bring, on average, $10,300 to the local economy. This calculation includes items ranging from food and lodging to gasoline, clothing, and entertainment. Just like their PSU counterparts, the 200 FSCC students taking classes on PSU's campus also shop in the city's retail outlets, eat in local restaurants, and purchase goods and services at Pittsburg vendors at that same $10,300 per-student rate. Using that rate, the direct economic impact of the FSCC–PSU partnership is over $2 million annually. Not included in that calculation is a multiplier that would take into account the ripple effect those dollars have throughout the local and regional economy. Using a common economic development multiplier of 1.75, the impact of those direct dollars would now become over $3.6 million—a significant source of economic power for a community of 14,000 citizens and a small retail base.

In addition to direct economic impact by the students who participate in this cooperative program, FSCC is investing in the Pittsburg community with other programs. Fort Scott operates a satellite campus in downtown Pittsburg that hosts the college's cosmetology and business programs. The presence of these programs is welcomed by both PSU and the downtown merchants. It represents just another example of FSCC investing in Pittsburg and partnering with PSU.

**Political Leverage.** Being located in a remote corner of the state can sometimes be challenging politically. In Kansas, political power is centered on the I-70 corridor that extends from Johnson County on the east (Kansas City metropolitan area) to Topeka approximately sixty-five miles west. Both Fort Scott and Pittsburg are geographically and politically removed from that corridor. For this reason, the partnership between the two institutions brings advantages to both in the area of political influence and leverage. KBOR is responsible for the oversight of the state's six public universities and coordination of the state's twenty-five community and technical colleges. PSU is one of these public universities and FSCC, though actually governed by a local board of trustees, has its academic programs coordinated by KBOR. In the past, members of the KBOR have bemoaned the lack of cooperation between the state's four-year universities and two-year community and technical colleges. A bright spot in that coordination effort, however, has been the Fort Scott–Pittsburg State relationship. The cooperative effort of these two institutions is often touted not only by KBOR, but also by legislators and state departments as a model of cooperation that saves the taxpayers money and eases the transition for students from a community college to a university. Such positive attention in the corridors of power in Topeka is priceless and gives both Fort Scott and Pittsburg State another talking point to share with elected officials about how their institutions are trying to make things better for Kansans.

## Other Benefits of the Relationship

Aside from the larger, more visible benefits to each institution, additional benefits have evolved over time as the relationship between FSCC and PSU has developed. Most of these added benefits have occurred not in discussions between the academic leaders of both campuses, but between other administrators who, observing how well the academic side of the house partnered with the other institution, identified ways for their programs to find a new and willing partner.

**Joint Marketing Efforts.** FSCC and PSU have been forced by demographic changes in Southeast Kansas to look beyond their traditional catchment areas to find new students. For Fort Scott, this means looking farther up and down Highway 69 for students from adjoining counties. At PSU, this has meant outreach to Southwest Missouri, Northeast Oklahoma, and Northwest Arkansas. Both institutions have used a more aggressive marketing effort to find new students. A joint marketing program that incorporates the messages of both Fort Scott and Pittsburg State was instituted in 2009. This program, centered primarily on outdoor advertising, begins with a FSCC message, but at the bottom incorporates a message about how PSU is a proud partner with Fort Scott. This single statement speaks volumes to prospective students and parents. Such joint marketing efforts in strategic

NEW DIRECTIONS FOR HIGHER EDUCATION • DOI: 10.1002/he

areas have proven to be very successful for both institutions and have strengthened in the public's mind the close working relationship between Fort Scott and Pittsburg State.

**Lobbying.** Both the college and the university have lobbying efforts at the state level. At times, when issues arise that are of interest to both FSCC and PSU, the senior administration and lobbying professionals affiliated with each school come together to develop a strategy that is beneficial to both institutions. Again, because of our remote locale, any efficiencies that can be obtained for travel, message, and depth of contact by partnering benefits both schools.

**Citizens Bank Bowl.** Athletic competitions play a large role for both FSCC and PSU in the areas of student recruitment, community engagement, and visibility. Each institution has its own proud traditions and intense rivalries. At FSCC, the Greyhounds have become a football powerhouse in the National Junior College Athletic Association (NJCAA). In 2009, Fort Scott had the opportunity to play in a post-season bowl game hosted by the local community. Because the anticipated crowd was going to be so large, particularly because their opponent was a traditional contender from nearby Texas, Fort Scott needed a larger facility to host the bowl game. The athletic administration staff at both schools immediately saw an opportunity and partnered to bring the Citizens Bank Bowl to Carnie Smith Stadium at PSU. Carnie Smith Stadium is one of the premier NCAA Division II stadiums in the nation, boasting a seating capacity of over 10,000, twenty-two luxury boxes, new field turf playing surface, and one of the largest state-of-the-art video boards in the country. Putting these factors together made a partnership between FSCC and PSU a unique opportunity for the student athletes of the college and the local Pittsburg business community. The inaugural Citizens Bank Bowl took place on December 6, 2009, and featured the number one and number two ranked junior college teams in the country, by default becoming the national championship game for junior college football that year. After being so successful in its first year, the game was again played in 2010 at PSU, and plans are to continue the event in 2011.

**KBOR Performance Agreement.** Pursuant to Kansas Senate Bill 647, both FSCC and PSU have formalized performance agreements with KBOR. This system of accountability and measurement is designed to ensure the academic and programmatic quality of all Kansas postsecondary institutions. Both institutions submitted predictable goals in all areas of academic operation including student performance, progress toward degrees, new or enhanced degree programs, diversity, etc. In addition, FSCC and PSU had the opportunity to write one another into their performance agreements. This reinforced in the minds of the nine regents and board staff the quality and sustainability of this relationship and how closely aligned these two institutions are in their pursuit of quality academic programs for students and quality of student life on both campuses.

NEW DIRECTIONS FOR HIGHER EDUCATION • DOI: 10.1002/he

## Conclusion

The Shared Campus Program is a best-practices model for collaboration between a university and community college. Considerable statewide attention has been paid to both institutions in recognition of the Shared Campus Program. Students who participate in this program clearly benefit as they transfer to PSU at a higher rate than from other two-year colleges in the state, and their success rate upon entering PSU is greater. Likely this is because of the seamless transition in all areas of a student's academic and social life that has been created by the Shared Campus Program. Other community colleges and universities across the country could benefit from adopting this type of partnership approach because it benefits both the partner institutions and the students themselves.

*CLAYTON N. TATRO is the President of Fort Scott Community College.*

*J. BRADFORD HODSON is the Vice President for University Advancement at Pittsburg State University.*

NEW DIRECTIONS FOR HIGHER EDUCATION • DOI: 10.1002/he

**5**

*Indiana University uses technology and knowledge management to provide abundant leveraged IT support.*

# Knowledge Sourcing in IT Support Services

*Sue B. Workman*

Indiana University (IU) provides great support for the technology our community needs to teach, learn, and conduct research. Rather than limiting support by defining a rigid support matrix, IU has chosen instead to utilize knowledge management technology to provide self-service for repetitive information technology (IT) questions, and focus precious human resources on issues that are new or that need logical intervention.

You may have heard of crowdsourcing, community sourcing, and open sourcing. At IU, we are knowledge sourcing, a form of intelligent crowdsourcing. "Crowdsourcing is a distributed problem-solving and production model. Problems are broadcast to an unknown group of solvers in the form of an open call for solutions. Users—also known as the crowd—typically form into online communities, and the crowd submits solutions. The crowd also sorts through the solutions, finding the best ones" (Wikipedia Contributors, 2010). The idea behind knowledge sourcing is to collect and distribute the knowledge of the community to gain efficiency and effectiveness. Our goal is to apply crowdsourcing for a particular IT support solution, that is, to eliminate repetitive problem solving for known issues; provide consistent answers; and maintain data in a single repository for editing, updating, and reuse. In short, we want to use technology for what it does best—repetitive use—and save our valuable human resources for problems that are either new or require human intervention. Although knowledge management can apply to any content, our goal is a system for IT self-help.

New Directions for Higher Education, no. 153, Spring 2011 © Wiley Periodicals, Inc.
Published online in Wiley Online Library (wileyonlinelibrary.com) • DOI: 10.1002/he.424

## The Knowledge Base and Self-Service at Indiana University

In the early 1980s, IU's IT Support Center (part of University Information Technology Services, or UITS) was suffering from high turnover and an ever-growing demand for service. The Center tended to hire large numbers of student employees who needed weeks of training. The natural student turnover required continual hiring and training, which are both time-consuming and expensive. We needed a solution that would keep knowledge from walking out the door, and save us from recreating it repeatedly. We needed tools that put answers at consultants' fingertips, so they could be productive without being trained on every possible subject or situation.

The first online IU Knowledge Base (KB) was established in about 1988. Back then it was a directory of files that consultants could browse for answers—an effective alternative to repeatedly re-solving problems and getting inconsistent results. The consultants who used it to answer email queries found the early KB especially helpful since they could cut and paste.

In the early 1990s, we moved this directory of files to Gopher, which allowed for full-text searching. We thought we had died and gone to heaven. Just a few months later, we heard about the World Wide Web, and the Gopher version became an albatross. Using the web, the world could search the KB at http://kb.iu.edu. Long before it was the norm for Microsoft and Apple, and more than a decade before Google became a household word, IU had self-service. We no longer needed a person to answer a question. In Fiscal Year 2009–2010, the IU KB received more than 29 million searches and contained more than 15,800 documents. Support Center consultants still use the KB to capture solutions. Of itself, the KB says, "Knowledge Management staff work with approximately 100 service providers and subject experts from departments and units across all eight campuses to identify, collect, deliver, and maintain both internal and external content in the Knowledge Base repository. This content functions as source material reused in other online information services and help systems, including most of the content in the UITS web space (http://uits.iu.edu), the TeraGrid Knowledge Base (https://www.teragrid.org/web/user-support/kb), and the Sakai Knowledge Base (https://www.indiana.edu/~sakaikb." (For more about the Indiana University Knowledge Base, see http://kb.iu.edu/data/aovp.html.)

### A Focus on Cost Effectiveness

As machines proliferated, demand grew, people used more devices per capita, and everything needed some sort of network connection, the IU KB enabled IU to leverage staff resources to provide even more online support. Personal support is expensive, even with a continually refreshed population of student employees who are smart and willing to work for a modest wage. This is reflected in IU's annual IT cost and quality scorecard, which has presented the costs of individual services since the 1995–1996 academic year.

New Directions for Higher Education • DOI: 10.1002/he

For example, in Fiscal Year 2009–2010, the 24/7 IT Support Center handled 218,000 contacts at a fully loaded cost to the university of about $11.32 per phone call, $12.17 per email message, $10.77 per chat, and $10.73 for walk-in service. During this same period, the KB had over 25 million searches at just over $.06 each. So even if someone did 10 searches for an answer (highly unlikely), the total cost at $.60 is markedly lower than the cost of a single personal contact. IU's costs compare especially favorably with those in corporate environments, where support staff is typically professionals with higher salaries and benefits.

We often think of IT support as a person-to-person interaction with a warm and fuzzy outcome. That is not always the case. On the first day of classes in 2010, the Support Center received over 2,000 contacts, many of which were repetitive questions from new students, parents, or faculty. In such conditions, and even with all their customer service training, consultants repeating the answer for the hundredth time may be worn out, omit something, or sound irritated. A machine, on the other hand, is consistent every time, unbothered by a queue or faltering energy levels. Wise division of labor does everyone good. When we use technology to help run our business, we let it do what it does best—the repetitive, and we leave for humans what they do best—the troubleshooting, teaching, and discovery.

The KB serves as a single economical and authoritative information repository. It proves the maxim, "Create once—use many times." Beyond answers to searches, the KB feeds other web pages, newsletters, message boards, and even help information in IU's community-source learning management system (Sakai). Faculty can put KB links in their coursework. When the information changes (and it always does), the link updates automatically.

## The Cost of Good Data

A knowledge system is only as good as its upkeep. Incorrect information is worse than no information. When searchers encounter out-of-date or incorrect answers, trust is broken, and it is doubtful they will ever come back. That is why you need excellent management, review processes and procedures, and tools to keep information current. No matter what system you use for a knowledge management system, you must continually cull, review, and correct the information. Extend this principle, and at some point it costs more to maintain content than to create it.

How is KB content created? The idea for content might come from support personnel, technical engineers, or interested faculty and staff. One of IU's eight Knowledge Management staff—working under standard operating procedures as strict as in any government agency—creates the content and metadata, assigns an owner and review cycle, gets technical approval, and then makes the content live to the appropriate audience. The audience might include such delimited groups as a particular school, department, or group;

or the Support Center consultants who use the content. Over the years, IU has become so expert at this process that its seasoned staff can publish a KB article in less than half an hour. At $.06 per search, that is a bargain.

But IT changes, and everything changes. Today a plethora of technology on our campuses does not support the enterprise or the teaching, learning, and research communities. Think of the entertainment gadgets students bring to dorm rooms; the technology in our vehicles, such as Microsoft Sync; and the new smartphones and devices that appear almost daily. Then factor in all the home network choices, printing devices, storage devices, and cloud services. How do we support all this?

Editors are a finite resource. In a typical week, the eight Knowledge Management staff at IU typically touch an average of 200 documents on technology that IT experts judge useful to the IU community. There is no way this staff could provide information about all these devices and services on their own. However, we are also surrounded by a very talented and technologically savvy community. Put these two together, and what do you get? Crowdsourcing 101.

Wikipedia defines *crowdsourcing* as a ". . . distributed problem-solving and production model." It refers to the term as ". . . a neologistic portmanteau of 'crowd' and 'outsourcing,' first coined by Jeff Howe in a June 2006 *Wired* magazine article, 'The Rise of Crowdsourcing'." Howe (2006) goes on to state that when cheap electronics flooded the market, consumers got more tech-savvy. If a company leverages this expertise, says Howe, "It's not outsourcing; it's crowdsourcing."

So how do we verify information from just anyone? Surely, I am contradicting myself. First, I call bad information worse than no information, and then I talk about crowdsourcing, which would seem to encourage all kinds of inconsistency and incorrectness. Yet there is good information in the crowd.

But how do you separate the wheat from the chaff? How do you provide the community with information that may be helpful, but inconsistent, and that may use incorrect metadata? How do you discern between information that is just plain wrong and information carefully authored by an authoritative staff and process? Wikipedia appears to have solved this dilemma, and even become a somewhat trusted resource—despite information changing on the fly and appearing in incomplete and flawed forms.

Would this work in a university setting? Are we putting our trusted reputation on the line if we encourage content editing by eighteen-year-olds? What will they add? What will the faculty and staff add? What about pornography? What if the anonymous "they" ruin our so carefully constructed content? Wikipedia has the world to create, correct, maintain, and curate content. We have a university of 130,000. Is 130,000 a large enough sample to crowdsource and maintain a credible repository of content? What if Professor Smith just has it in for Professor Jones and deliberately messes up her content? Should faculty and student information be treated equally? Will anyone care? What if no one contributes? Should this be just IT information? Should we open this up to information from the library, admissions, and physical plant? What if we open it up, and "they" ruin everything we have worked so hard to create? Is crowdsourcing really what we want to do? How will we know?

So many questions without definitive answers!

We worry too much. But, in the end, is that not the job of IT support—to worry, then proactively tackle problems before they impact the work of our university?

## The Test at Indiana University

Indiana University decided to take an intermediary step to learn how a totally open crowdsourced environment would work in our community. To pilot our ideas, we created an additional system alongside the KB called the Knowledge Commons. The IU Knowledge Commons (https://wiki.uits.iu.edu) is an online, collaborative wiki environment for sharing information in support of the IU community. We wanted to build quickly in order to learn, so we traded "bells and whistles" for functionality we already had. The system is built on top of Confluence and provides a large set of commonly accessed KB articles. Various schools, organizations, and departments have also set up their own spaces and editing environments.

Will mass editing corrupt our information? Here is how we are handling the "crowd." Anyone can read any page. However, only those with authenticated credentials (shown by logging in with an IU network ID) can create new pages and edit existing ones, comment on any page, add labels to any page, submit feedback, or create a community of interest. Knowledge Commons entries are attributed to their sources, so searchers can easily distinguish between material submitted by the community and content delivered with certitude by UITS.

## Lessons to Date

We are learning from this experience. We find that only a small portion of the community will create, edit, or publish information. Many schools and organizations want to have their own space that is individual to their constituency. We are concluding that crowdsourcing within our own community may not deliver the rich support resource we wanted.

So we looked at a different point of leverage. IU desperately needed to modernize the Knowledge Base code. The KB over time became a mission-critical system at IU. Nevertheless, we could not deliver abundant support without a self-service tool. Other problems persisted. The KB was developed over a couple of decades by various individuals, so sustaining it was becoming

New Directions for Higher Education • DOI: 10.1002/he

a person-dependent task. The editing environment was antiquated, and we wanted new features.

IU is a long-standing believer in open and community source software. So we turned first to the higher education community to jointly develop code that could be shared. We hosted staff from eleven interested schools, and after a two-day discussion, a light bulb went off. Yes, we could share *code*, but the real leverage point was to share *content*. After a very unscientific but independent analysis, we concluded that we could share about 60 percent of the content we were writing, whether that content was 15,800 documents at IU or a FAQ (frequently asked questions) of 1,500 documents at a private school.

We may need small tweaks to make content institution-dependent, but installing a virtual private network at IU or at another institution is much the same. Perhaps we have a database of institution-dependent information from which other schools can draw and build on-the-fly documents with their own look and feel. This "above-campus" (Wheeler and Waggener, 2009) service and content sharing by multiple systems may be the way to really leverage our support systems. This may be the knowledge-sourcing golden nugget.

## Kuali, A Starting Point

Thus emerged the Kuali IT Support incubation project (see http://kb.iu.edu/data/azlc.html). The first model in this community source project is the Knowledge Management System (see http://kb.iu.edu/data/azgk.html), which will be coded in the Kuali framework and thus sustainable. We visualized institutions writing their own features and submitting them to the community, or implementing this as a hosted service in which content is shared, re-used, leveraged, and maintained in a single above-the-campus location. Just at this critical point, the economic crisis hit. Indiana University and the University of Hawaii are currently partnering to develop this system, and seeking partners to bring this dream to reality. We are inviting other schools to join the effort, then benefit from a system for developing, managing, and sharing content that, once complete, will be worth millions of dollars.

## The Final Word

Crowdsourcing experiments with the IU community have been moderately successful. The next phase is to leverage the higher education community and share content creation and maintenance above-campus (Wheeler and Waggener, 2009). This system is not limited by topic. Although IU is focusing on IT information, this process and system will work for any type of information.

# References

Howe, J. "The Rise of Crowdsourcing." *Wired*, June 2006. Retrieved September 13, 2010, from http://www.wired.com/wired/archive/14.06/crowds.html.

IU Knowledge Base Contributors. "What Is the History of the Knowledge Base?" Indiana University Knowledge Base. Retrieved September 13, 2010, from http://kb.iu.edu/data/acjq.html.

Wheeler, B., and Waggener, S. "Above-Campus Services: Shaping the Promise of Cloud Computing for Higher Education." *EDUCAUSE Review*, 2009, 44(6). Retrieved September 13, 2010, from http://www.educause.edu/EDUCAUSE+Review/EDUCAUSE ReviewMagazineVolume44/AboveCampusServicesShapingtheP/185222.

Wikipedia Contributors. "Crowdsourcing." *Wikipedia*, The Free Encyclopedia. Retrieved September 13, 2010, from http://en.wikipedia.org/wiki/Crowdsourcing.

*SUE B. WORKMAN is the Associate Vice President for Communication and Support in the Office of the Vice President for Information Technology at Indiana University.*

6

*A new Health Sciences undergraduate major created a need for innovative support services on a recently established campus.*

# The Student Success Coach

*Claudia Neuhauser, Kendra Weber*

An innovative position, a Student Success Coach, was created in response to a newly developed undergraduate-degree program on the recently established University of Minnesota Rochester campus. Student Success Coaches serve as the link between the academic and student affairs sides of the campus. They interact closely with students and faculty to provide prompt feedback and support on academic and personal matters, and in turn foster active student engagement in the learning and development process.

## Background for the University of Minnesota Rochester Campus

In December 2006, the University of Minnesota established a new campus in Rochester, Minnesota, the University of Minnesota Rochester (UMR), to meet the demands of the research-based economy of Rochester's industries, especially in health care and biotechnology. The new campus was recommended by the Rochester Higher Education Development Committee (RHEDC), which was appointed by the Governor of Minnesota to develop a plan to meet the educational and research needs in the Rochester area. The report was delivered in January 2006 (Rochester Higher Education Development Committee, 2006).

The UMR's new programs are being developed in the biosciences, health sciences, and biotechnology. The first program that was developed is the all-university, interdisciplinary graduate program in Biomedical Informatics and Computational Biology that admitted its first graduate students in fall 2008 and has since grown to about thirty students. The second program developed was the Bachelor of Science (BS) in Health Sciences (BSHS), which admitted its first cohort of fifty-seven students in fall 2009 and is expected to grow to about 250 freshmen per year over the next three

New Directions for Higher Education, no. 153, Spring 2011 © Wiley Periodicals, Inc.
Published online in Wiley Online Library (wileyonlinelibrary.com) • DOI: 10.1002/he.425

to four years. A third program, a BS in Health Professions (BSHP), will start in fall 2011 and will be a junior-admitting program with tracks in five allied health programs. These programs form synergistic partnerships with two organizations that have a strong presence in Rochester: the Mayo Clinic, a world leader in clinical practice and biomedical research, and IBM, the largest industrial research organization in the world focused on information technology.

With the arrival in fall 2007 of the first chancellor, Dr. Stephen Lehmkuhle, the direction for the four-year undergraduate program was set: a rigorous curriculum based on learning principles emerging from the cognitive and behavioral sciences (National Research Council, 2000) in a technology-enhanced learning environment would prepare students for a broad array of health-related careers. A new faculty model and the use of Student Success Coaches would provide a supportive environment for meeting student learning and development outcomes. Ongoing, technology-supported assessment would personalize learning and help identify academic short-comings before they result in student failure. To take a tour of the early days of the program, we invite the reader to peruse the article by Glenn (2009).

## Developing the Student Success Coach Model

The Student Success Coach program, led by Assistant Vice Chancellor for Student Affairs, Kendra Weber, started with one Student Success Coach in fall 2009 and added a second coach in fall 2010. Student Success Coaches work closely with BSHS students to provide support for academic and personal challenges, and are in close contact with faculty in the Center for Learning Innovation (CLI) to identify individual and common issues that students are facing within the curriculum.

The CLI, the academic home of the BSHS and BSHP, was established in 2007 and houses the faculty and postdoctoral fellows for these degree programs. The director of this center and vice chancellor for academic affairs responsible for development of these degree programs is Dr. Claudia Neuhauser. As UMR has no departments, CLI houses different disciplines, thus enabling the development of an integrated curriculum across disciplinary boundaries and an integrated assessment system across the entire curriculum.

The role of the Student Success Coach in the CLI is based on pedagogical theory. For example, Keeling (2004) identifies some of the ways that a traditionally structured curriculum neglects to address issues of individual student learning by emphasizing the "transfer of information" without regard to the relevance or application of that knowledge within the student's life context, which includes what the student knows about herself, values, and believes to be true. To include a student's life context in the learning process, Keeling espouses the concept of transformative education, which "places the student's reflective processes at the core of the learning experience" and expands the goal of education to include the "evolution of multidimensional identity" (p. 9). Student affairs practitioners are encouraged to respond to this broader understanding of learning and learning outcomes by "mapping" and supporting learning everywhere it takes place on today's campuses, and by intentionally creating, implementing, and assessing student learning outcomes.

In addition, Chickering and Gamson (1987) identified "seven principles for good practice in undergraduate education," including encouraging contact between students and faculty, developing cooperation among students, using active learning techniques, giving prompt feedback, emphasizing time on task, communicating high expectations, and respecting diverse talents and ways of learning. Finally, Astin's (1999) theory of student involvement indicates that for student growth and development to take place, a student must actively engage in his environment; this involvement can be gauged both by the amount of time devoted to the "object" (learning experience) as well as the seriousness with which the object was approached. Astin also maintains, "the amount of student learning and personal development associated with any educational program is directly proportional to the quality and quantity of student involvement in that program" (p. 519). Indeed, the effectiveness of any educational practice or policy is related to the degree to which it produces student involvement.

To put into practice these recommendations and observations from the body of scholarship on student development and to implement a learning outcomes approach to student support, Ms. Weber and Nathan Tesch, UMR Assistant Director for Student Life, created an outline identifying the components required in student and academic support before the BSHS curriculum had even begun to be developed. These included:

- Each student's needs are to be addressed in a holistic manner.
- Support is provided for the academic curriculum by integrating academic advising, career exploration, and academic support services into a model whereby students have opportunities to utilize the services they need to be successful.
- Students will be provided with multiple opportunities to take advantage of professional development and support resources.

Ms. Weber and Mr. Tesch then determined that the best method for delivering these components was to develop a professional position that would integrate the challenge and support functions identified by Sanford (1962) as essential for student success, with the learning outcomes–based approach to educational experiences. While envisioning the qualities such a professional would possess and the responsibilities that would make up the job description for this person, we referred to this position often as "somewhat like a coach": part encourager, part enforcer. In the end, we determined that in fact this was the proper description, with a couple of modifiers; a job description was developed and a search underway for a Student Success Coach. (See the Appendix for the job description.)

NEW DIRECTIONS FOR HIGHER EDUCATION • DOI: 10.1002/he

The Student Success Coach model assumes a great deal of interaction between the coach and the faculty, as well as the coach and students, without supplanting the necessary contact directly between students and faculty. Coaches and faculty participate together in meetings to appraise each other of larger issues. Individual meetings between faculty and coaches address issues of specific students and trends in and outside of the classroom. A software package is currently under development that will allow faculty to "flag" students who experience academic difficulties. Coaches have access to the flags and can identify students who struggle before serious academic issues arise. The flags will not replace communication between faculty and coaches, but rather provide a communication tool that informs coaches across courses without the need for all faculty to know about their students' performance in all their courses. Limiting faculty access to students' performance issues helps prevent labeling students as poor performers before they even start a course with a new instructor.

## A New Faculty Model

In addition to the Student Success Coach, a nontraditional faculty model was developed that features three types of academic professionals and fosters a project-based and community-integrated learning environment.

- "Design faculty," with deep grounding in their disciplines and a strong interest in the science of learning, develop a cohesive curriculum based on insights from the cognitive and behavioral sciences. Design faculty are either on regular tenured or on tenure-track appointments and engage in both research and the delivery of the curriculum. Those with tenure-track appointments have the possibility of promotion to tenured rank based on performance.
- "Student-based faculty" work closely with design faculty on implementation and delivery of the curriculum and are available to students for small group or one-on-one help. Student-based faculty are typically full-time members of the team, though not on tenure track, and provide year-to-year continuity in the classroom. During classroom projects, multiple student-based faculty across disciplines may be simultaneously in the classroom to facilitate learning.
- Postdoctoral fellows spend two or three years as "faculty in training," honing their teaching skills in a project-based curriculum and engaging with design faculty in research on learning.

In fall 2009, the CLI had five design faculty, three student-based faculty, and three postdoctoral fellows. It grew to 10 design faculty, 8.75 student-based faculty, and 3 postdoctoral fellows by fall 2010. The total number of faculty and postdoctoral fellows is expected to grow to about fifty in the next three to four years.

## Integration of Curriculum and Campus Experiences in the BSHS

The creation of a new campus provides an exciting opportunity to create a curriculum and co-curricular learning opportunities in an intentional manner, which builds on insights from student development and teaching and learning scholarship, and in turn contributes to the scholarship. The starting point has been the vision of the CLI that serves as a steady compass during this development: "The Center for Learning Innovation (CLI) is a single academic unit where faculty across disciplines deliver a synergistic program in the health sciences that prepares students for a wide variety of health careers, including health professions, graduate studies in health-related programs, and careers in the bioscience industry. The CLI promotes a learner-centered, technology-enhanced, concept-driven, and community-integrated learning environment. Through ongoing assessment of student achievement, the CLI aspires to personalize learning, establish data-driven research on learning, and continuously improve the curriculum" (CLI, 2010).

Students majoring in the BSHS receive an integrated education across the life and health sciences, the physical sciences, the quantitative sciences, the social sciences, and the humanities. A key feature of the program is that the degree program provides students with the flexibility to explore different career options. Students will share a common curriculum during the first two years that provides the basic science and liberal education background needed to succeed in careers in the biotechnology sector and the health sciences. Career advising and student development is integrated into the curriculum to broaden a student's perspective of career paths in the context of the curriculum and to prepare students for the increasingly complex work environment they will enter upon graduation. The final two years of the BSHS curriculum allow for capstone experiences outside of regular coursework, including internships in industry or research projects in academic or industry laboratories.

Campuswide student learning and development outcomes define what a student will be able to do after completion of a UMR undergraduate-degree program and provide achievement goals for student development. To measure learning and development outcomes, curriculum and campus experiences are being designed based on measurable learning and development objectives. These objectives provide specific goals of learning experiences, both in and out of the classroom, including what a student should be able to demonstrate (know, do, or value) as a result of engaging in the learning experience, and are mapped to learning and development outcomes. Institutional effectiveness can be demonstrated through learning and development outcomes by means of identifying learning objectives, and collecting and analyzing the data, which provide the evidence of impact on the students. Learning and development outcomes are thus viewed as the cumulative achievement over the four years, and goals can be set for each year to guide students.

## Conclusion

We have found the Student Success Coach model to be particularly effective in implementing Chickering and Gamson's (1987) best practices of prompt feedback: the coach is able to converse with students who are just beginning to struggle, before even a midterm academic report might indicate the need for intervention, emphasizing time on task and communicating high expectations. Each student is required to meet with his or her coach throughout the semester, more often for students who are encountering academic or personal difficulties. The coach has been able to help craft study plans for students in academic distress, and to allow students on academic probation to continue toward their degree with additional oversight and support.

Students are also encouraged to connect with the coach when things are going well, and to keep the coach informed of plans for additional learning experiences (internships, study abroad, etc.) or changes in career plans and goals. The Student Success Coach model de-emphasizes the need for students to receive permission from the coach (as an advisor) to enroll, or change courses, and instead creates a relationship that provides guidance and support at multiple interactions, both formal and informal. This is to foster what Schlossberg (1989) calls a student's sense of "mattering": the belief that someone else finds one important and worthy of attention.

Due to the exclusive focus on health sciences at UMR, some students have determined during their first year that the campus is not the right fit for pursuing a degree in other fields. Exit interviews conducted with these students before they left UMR revealed a strong sentiment from each that they valued the interaction and support they received from the Student Success Coach, and in fact were concerned that their new campuses would not have such a position. More data collection will be done to determine the effectiveness of this model over time, but early indications suggest that providing a Student Success Coach is helping meet the academic and developmental needs of students at UMR.

## References

Astin, A. W. 1999. "Student Involvement: A Developmental Theory for Higher Education." *Journal of College Student Personnel*, 40, 518–529.

Center for Learning Innovation (CLI), University of Minnesota Rochester. 2010."Vision." Accessed August 24, 2010, http://www.r.umn.edu/research/cli/index.htm.

Chickering, A. W., and Gamson, Z. F. 1987."Seven Principles for Good Practice in Undergraduate Education." *AAHE Bulletin*, 39(7), 3–7.

Glenn, D. 2009."Learning Goes Under a Microscope." *The Chronicle of Higher Education*, November 6, pp. A1, A8, A10.

Keeling, R. P., (ed.) 2004. *Learning Reconsidered: A Campus-wide Focus on the Student Experience*. Accessed August 24, 2010, www.myacpa.org/pub/documents/Learning Reconsidered.doc.

National Research Council. 2000. *How People Learn*. Washington, DC: National Research Council.

Rochester Higher Education Development Committee. 2006. "Report to Governor Tim Pawlenty and the Minnesota Legislature." Accessed January 10, 2011, http://www.r .umn.edu/downloads/RHEDC/Other%20PDF's/RHEDCreportFinal.pdf.

Sanford, N. 1962. *The American College*. New York: Wiley.

Schlossberg, N. K. 1989. "Marginality and Mattering: Key Issues in Building Community." *New Directions for Student Services*, 48, 5–15.

CLAUDIA NEUHAUSER *is Vice Chancellor for Academic Affairs and Director of the Center for Learning Innovation at the University of Minnesota Rochester.*

KENDRA WEBER *is Assistant Vice Chancellor for Student Affairs at the University of Minnesota Rochester.*

NEW DIRECTIONS FOR HIGHER EDUCATION • DOI: 10.1002/he

# Appendix

## UMR Student Success Coach Position Description

### Summary of Position

The student coach position is based on traditional academic advising philosophy but is designed for a new institutional and curricular model. UMR is in the process of creating an exciting new model where faculty research student learning, greater amounts of data are used to guide the student experience, courses are based on interaction and examples rather than lecture, and the interdisciplinary curriculum is directly relevant to subsequent courses and career paths. UMR will promote undergraduate student success by enhancing students' connection to the university and creating a bridge to the wider world beyond the university by means of career exploration, community engagement, and special learning opportunities.

Student coaches participate in three major areas of responsibility: academic advising and student advocacy; project development and management; and professional development, service, and research. Working directly with faculty and other staff, the coach advises students throughout their collegiate careers (from matriculation to graduation) to ensure students' career exploration activities, academic progress, and co-curricular involvement will prepare them to achieve their academic and career goals.

### Duties and Responsibilities

*Academic Advising & Student Advocacy*

Help students complete their academic studies, graduate in a timely manner, and be prepared to meet the challenges of their next endeavor by providing information, teaching skills, and providing access to resources.

- Lead and mentor students through the process of formulating personalized educational plans and developing strategies for academic success; improve students' skills in these areas through training and selecting and providing resources; encourage the use of tools available to students, such as GradPlanner
- Monitor student progress toward graduation in order to intervene, advise, and help students meet and overcome academic and personal obstacles; make appropriate university and community referrals based on individual student needs; extract, analyze, and report on student progress utilizing available databases and resources (e.g., APAS, PeopleSoft, UM Reports, iSEAL)
- Facilitate student interaction with administrative and recurring functions such as registration and graduation application
- Direct students through capstone proposal process, from initial concept to formal proposal to completion and reflection on experience; evaluate

NEW DIRECTIONS FOR HIGHER EDUCATION • DOI: 10.1002/he

suitability of capstone proposal before student makes formal presentation to faculty

- Plan, develop content for, and conduct informational group meetings, e.g., for orientation/registration, introduction to capstone proposal process
- Function as a liaison with faculty to ensure appropriate recourses are available, for example, evaluating, recommending, and selecting software, tutoring aids, or peer mentoring programs; act as an intermediary between students, faculty, and community experts regarding FERPA protected issues
- Evaluate need for, plan, and develop informational materials used to advise students
- Timely completion of administrative duties such as recommending action on petition requests and degree clearance to the registrar, developing probation contracts with students
- Other duties and responsibilities as assigned or required

*Project Development & Management*

In addition to their primary advising assignment, student coaches will undertake additional project(s) that will contribute significantly to the student experience. Projects will be assigned and selected based on personal interest and skills as well as institutional needs.

- Serve as lead for select student affairs initiatives and programs such as study abroad, student organizations, orientation, commencement, parent communication, student activities, student government, and other special events, based on campus need and individual interest
- Participate in efforts to improve retention rates, four-year graduation rates, and student satisfaction; responsibilities may include project chair, recommending course of action, pilot project management
- Design and implement student development activities based on assessment data and best practices.
- Track and summarize data to analyze trends and make recommendations for practice improvement and creation of new practices in consideration of audience

**Professional Development, Service, and Research**
Engage in professional development, service activities, and research related to the student learning, student success, academic advising, and student affairs profession, both within the University of Minnesota community and beyond.

- Contribute to the strategic planning process for the Office of Student Affairs by proactively examining outcomes, developing new process, and making recommendations for improvement of services and resources

- Actively contribute to the improvement of written and electronic advising information and materials by updating existing materials and developing new material
- Continue professional development and scholarly activity in the field of academic advising to maintain knowledge of trends and best practices (e.g., membership in professional associations, attendance at conferences and seminars, write and publish articles, serve on teams and collaborate with other professional groups, etc.)
- Serve on Student Affairs, Campus, and University-wide committees or groups

### Required Qualifications

Master's degree and one year of college-level advising or teaching experience; or bachelor's degree plus three years advising college or college bound students.

The successful candidate will possess a commitment to equal opportunity and diversity issues, including the ability to work with a diverse student, staff, and faculty population; the ability to innovate; the ability to learn and disseminate detailed information using a high level of interpersonal skills; excellent oral and written communication skills; the ability to be self-motivated, work in collaborative, team environment, and respond well to supervision; excellent time management and organization skills; strong computer skills within the Windows environment to include word processing, e-mail, and database manipulation; a demonstrated ability to work with complex systems in a fast-paced and structured setting; and the ability to multi-task and pay attention to details.

### Preferred Qualifications

Master's, PhD, or equivalent in student personnel, counseling psychology, counseling, or related area. Three or more years of relevant higher education advising experience.

Experience with career enrichment programming.

Experience advising students interested in health care professions.

Experience tracking and interpreting data relevant to their work and using that information for work and process improvement.

Familiarity with PeopleSoft system.

A commitment to knowledge creation and research in higher education.

# 7

*Western Michigan University responded to the unique and growing needs of military and veteran students by creating an office that spearheaded a move to engage the entire academic community.*

# A Proactive Approach to Serving Military and Veteran Students

*Tracey L. Moon, Geraldine A. Schma*

With the introduction of the Post 9/11 GI Bill in August 2009, Veterans Affairs anticipated a 25-percent increase in the number of service members who would enroll in higher education (Student Affairs Leadership Council, 2009). Between fall 2005 and spring 2010 semesters, Western Michigan University (WMU; Kalamazoo, MI) experienced a 43-percent boom, from just over 300 to just fewer than 500 students representing this population (Western Michigan University, 2010). In anticipation of and response to the unique needs of this special group of adult learners, Western Michigan University created an office to offer resources and support to military and veteran students by coordinating student services providers from across campus and the local community. The philosophies and practices of the WMU administration, faculty, and staff have resulted in 2009 WMU earning recognition as a "Military Friendly Institution" by two different national publications (KMI Media Group, 2009; Victory Media, Inc., 2010). In this chapter, the authors present an overview of the history of the office and the development of the System of Care, the status of the office and programs, and goals for future development and services to meet the ongoing needs of military and veteran students on college campuses.

## Identifying the Need

Western Michigan University prides itself on a student body diverse in age, gender, and ethnicity. Because 28 percent of adult learners comprise the student population, an institutional mentality exists that recognizes and supports the multiple priorities and challenges that face these individuals. One component within this group is current and former service members (Western

NEW DIRECTIONS FOR HIGHER EDUCATION, no. 153, Spring 2011 © Wiley Periodicals, Inc.
Published online in Wiley Online Library (wileyonlinelibrary.com) • DOI: 10.1002/he.426

Michigan University, 2009). Therefore, in 2007, when the first wave of Iraq veterans returned to civilian life and sought college admission or readmission, staff and select faculty recognized the effects of those students' distinct behavior by reviewing transcripts and observing classroom behavior.

Students seeking readmission after midsemester deployments who failed to notify the university had a semester's worth of X's—X being the grade given to students who stop showing up to class early in a semester but never officially drop the course with the registrar's office—and those who did notify were out of sequence in their major. First-time students who submitted military transcripts for evaluation were granted few if any credits, and, in most cases, financial benefits lagged behind institutional due dates. Worse yet, reintegration for combat veterans proved extremely challenging. Not only did military experiences distance them from their much younger classmates, the effects of posttraumatic stress disorder (PTSD), traumatic brain injury (TBI), and depression impacted concentration and memory skills in ways that even the student couldn't understand (Student Affairs Leadership Council, 2009).

Soon, staff who worked with nontraditional students became concerned with the complexity and seriousness of issues faced by service members and alerted the administration who requested an analysis and recommendations for a solution and a commitment to be more "military friendly." *Military friendly* refers to the intentional efforts made by campuses to identify and remove barriers to the educational goals of veterans and create a smooth transition from military to college life (Strickley, 2009). The outcome of research and individual interviews was the creation in April 2007 of the Advocacy Office for Transfer Students and Military Affairs (recently renamed The Office of Veteran and Military Affairs) devoted to supporting the needs of current service members and veterans (Baron, 2007).

## System of Care

The success of the office rests on two guiding principles: listen to the soldiers and "everybody plays." A review of academic records identified that problems existed, but listening to the soldiers' stories and expressed frustrations identified specific problems and their origins. It immediately became evident that advocacy staff needed to support the many soldiers, but also to educate and engage the academic community. In such instances, usually the brightest and most committed volunteer, and fortunately this was no exception. Faculty and administrators in student affairs, health and human services, the unified clinics, and academic support units came together to form a military oversight committee to collaborate with the advocacy office to create a program known as the "System of Care." This concept allows a forum in which students and university staff could access resources to address most any personal or health issue a military student may face.

Thus, the principle of "everybody plays" was embraced. "Everybody plays" refers to the buy-in from faculty and staff to embrace and actively participate in the military friendly paradigm. Educational seminars given by Veterans Administration counselors, as well as presentations by the military advocate and student veterans themselves, provided insight into this unique population. They also had the desirable effect of creating opportunities for faculty, staff, and community members to step forward to express interest and offer their particular expertise.

Meanwhile, the "everybody plays" concept was expanded to the notion of a caring community that not only includes the System of Care, but also involves other areas that could address academic, social, or individual needs. A very critical component was the Military and Veterans Student Association (MVSA), which was one of the first student organizations to affiliate with the national Student Veterans of America (SVA). This organization is the official voice of student veterans and works closely with the military affairs office to address current and critical issues (SVA, 2010). Members also interface with local veterans groups, such as the American Legion, Veterans of Foreign Wars (VFW), and student groups from local and statewide veteran student organizations. Other caring community venues include community networks such as food banks, housing services, and family service agencies. Academic support services include academic departments, admissions, the registrar's office, and student services. Military support services originally included the VA hospital, the VA Administration, and state VA support groups and services, but has also grown to include installations from all branches of the military.

## Responding to the Need

Once the advocacy office was in place, listening and responding to the needs of the service members was top priority. One critical issue expressed by this population and verified by Strickley (2009) was the need for accurate and timely receipt of GI Bill benefits. WMU was already at the forefront of addressing this issue, as one full-time staff person in the registrar's office was designated as the certifying official for the university. This staff member's sole responsibility is to submit and monitor all GI Bill benefits with the Veterans Administration. Although that may not seem that impressive, at other institutions, the certifying official usually has other responsibilities within the department, therefore taking away from the focus on veterans.

**Military and Veteran Student Association.** According to the Student Affairs Leadership Council (2009), providing ways for veterans to connect with each other inside and outside the classroom is important and the Military and Veteran Student Association (MVSA) attempts to do just that.

This registered student organization allows for camaraderie for military and veteran students, including Reserve Officer Training Corps students and family members on WMU's campus. The MVSA office is accessible and welcoming, and it offers a voice to this population. In addition to providing support for students, its members strive to connect to the university community, as well as the local community. The MVSA sponsors a Veteran's Day Run from the campus to Ft. Custer National Cemetery. This event not only involves current students running, but also alumni, community members, and members of the Veterans Administration. The MVSA also supports the Marine Corps League's Toys for Tots and solicits donations for care packages to be sent to WMU students who are deployed. In addition, the MVSA partners with WMU Athletics for annual Veterans Appreciation football and hockey games to promote awareness. The MVSA also partners with Kalamazoo Valley Community College's student association and has created ties to veteran students wanting to eventually transfer to WMU.

**Veterans Administration.**  Although all military branches offer GI Bill benefit information during after-deployment debriefings, many soldiers are focused on getting home and back to their families and end up very confused about their benefits (Cook and Kim, 2009). To address this lack of understanding, WMU has asked the local Veterans Administration (VA) hospital to send the VA Transition Advocate to campus once a month to meet with students about any VA-related issue, but in particular, benefits. Despite the VA already being stressed, the VA director recognized the need and positive partnership and gave approval on a trial basis, allowing students to conveniently meet with someone in person on campus and have their questions answered (Student Affairs Leadership Council, 2009).

Another way the local VA collaborates with the university is via a PTSD Clinical Psychologist, a WMU alumni, who serves on the military oversight committee and has facilitated educational workshops on campus. Students have voiced an appreciation for having a VA presence on campus and veteran's publications indicate these types of partnerships are purposeful and beneficial for all involved (Student Affairs Leadership Council, 2009).

On a national level, WMU administration has given approval to participate in the VA Yellow Ribbon program since the program's inception in 2009 (US Department of Veterans Affairs, 2010). This is a voluntary financial commitment by the higher education institution to offer funding to veterans whose benefits do not completely cover their tuition and fees: the VA then matches these funds. To date, six WMU students have benefitted from this program (WMU, 2009).

**Additional Military Friendly Policies and Practices.**  Participation in proactive support included the highest level of campus leadership members and administration and a variety of campus department members.

**Financial.**  The Board of Trustees directed that some form of transitional support be provided to current and future deployed students. With the input of the financial aid office, the Returning Veterans Tuition Assistance program was developed. The RVTA program (Roland, 2007) awarded full tuition for the first semester. This not only relieved the stress caused by delayed payment but when monies were finally received, the veteran could apply them to the next semester, thus providing a continual safety net.

In addition, all students received in-state status for subsequent semesters. The Board of Trustees later extended in-state status to spouses and dependent family members (Davis, 2008). This practice was later adopted by all Michigan higher education institutions. The tuition assistance program was enthusiastically received by student veterans and is credited with spearheading WMU's recognition as a military friendly school and other supportive efforts on campus.

Formal procedures were established by the registrar that expedited the deployment process. When active-duty students are deployed, all they have to do to receive funds for fees, books, and tuition they have already paid is to provide the university with a copy of their orders. Students are allowed to withdraw or be granted incompletes, and user-friendly checklists identifying withdrawal and reentry processes were provided to the student.

Lastly, due to delayed benefit payment by the VA, students have the option to access an emergency loan through WMU to pay for expenses, such as books or housing. The registrar and accounts receivable office also started to identify military students who were waiting on the VA to pay tuition bills to make sure no holds were put on the students' accounts so that they were allowed to register for next semester classes without delay.

**Classes, communication, and graduation.** To keep deployed students connected to the campus and on the path to graduation, practices regarding registration, methods of communication, and graduation recognition were put in place to support them.

Many faculty responded positively to encouragement to work with deployed students to finish coursework expeditiously while in the field or immediately upon their return. Many creative responses by faculty have been and continue to be offered to provide continuity during deployments. A policy was implemented granting all deployed students priority registration prior to and for one year immediately following deployment, which helped students maintain programmatic sequence. As in the registrar's office, the admissions office designated one credit evaluator whose sole responsibility is to assess military transcripts by using clear documented criteria to award credit.

While in the field, military students are allowed to maintain student email accounts for up to one year to remain connected to the university. In response to the difficulty in determining the number of enrolled military students, the graduate, undergraduate, and readmission applications now contain a question requesting students to self-identify. This military status also allows military and veteran students to be identified and recognized during graduation ceremonies by being offered red, white, and blue honor cords to wear at commencement and being asked to stand by the president during the convocation (Student Affairs Leadership Council, 2009).

## Continue to Listen, Then Meet and Exceed Expectations

Although WMU has been on the forefront of being military friendly, a need for continuous improvement always exists. To do that, key staff members have attended conferences across the nation to network, learn from, and share successes with other institutions.

**Program Implementation.** At the Department of Defense Education Symposium in 2009, many excellent presenters shared information and ideas for effectively serving this population. For example, attendees learned about and subsequently applied for grants to increase the level of service to veterans on campus and to be educated about the effectiveness of first-year courses to address the transition from soldier to student (Anthony, 2009; Schupp, 2009). In response, a two-credit, transition course was approved by WMU academic administration and was offered for the first time during the fall 2010 semester. In addition, for the first time, a one-credit meditation course for veterans is being offered by a counseling faculty member who is also a veteran, to help meet the requests of students to learn how to better cope with the stress of going to school. The Student Affairs Leadership Council (2009) highly recommends offering an orientation program specifically for veterans where pertinent information is presented by key university contacts. When this concept was proposed to current military students, the reaction was positive; therefore, one has been offered at WMU at the beginning of the 2010–2011 school year.

**Military Students' Suggestions.** According to several publications and conversations with WMU military students, two main observations surfaced: (1) faculty and staff need additional training to be more sensitive to veterans on campus, and (2) military and veteran students need mentoring (Frantz and Asher, 2009, p. 48).

**University-wide training.** Despite offering webinars and speakers on campus to educate the campus community about military students on campus, students still voiced encountering some misperceptions about them (Frantz and Asher, 2009). The administration distributed a flier to all faculty, staff, and administrators across campus directing them to provide tools and resources when interacting with military students to best meet their needs. Informative presentations, offered in collaboration with the Office of Faculty Development and other administrative bodies on campus and delivered in steps, are planned, beginning with faculty and continuing through summer semesters and into the upcoming 2011–2012 academic year.

**Mentoring.** As a diverse and typically underserved population on college campuses, making connections to other military students is crucial (Strickley, 2009). WMU students have echoed that view and to meet the need, WMU is exploring two programs to implement. First, a faculty and staff mentoring program was developed that recommended that faculty and staff with any military background volunteer to mentor incoming, first-year military students.

This will allow for additional exposure and connection to the military affairs office by employees and will connect new students with people who are familiar with both the campus and the military perspective. Second, WMU is going to be participating with the Wounded Warrior Project, a nonprofit organization with a mission to honor and empower severely injured service members, which will also provide veteran education transition assistance through veteran students mentoring other veteran students (Wounded Warrior, 2010).

## Summary

As universities continue to experience an influx of military and veteran students utilizing their GI Bill benefits, faculty and staff will be asked to accommodate this traditionally underserved population. Western Michigan University has not only attempted to accommodate, but also to embrace service members who want to pursue higher education. Although implementing programs and policies may seem challenging in the beginning, the payoff in welcoming and providing services to ensure the success of this most deserving group will come not only in dollars, but also in the satisfaction and pride in knowing the university's employees did the right thing.

## References

Anthony, L. K. "Institutional Grants to Support Projects for Veterans for Veterans-Related Research." Presentation at Department of Defense Education Symposium, Atlanta. July 29, 2009.

Baron, J. 2007. "Advocacy Office Fills Important Need." *WMU News* Archive. Kalamazoo: Western Michigan University, September 14. http://www.wmich.edu/wmu/news/2007/09/033.html.

Cook, B. J., and Kim, Y. 2009. *From Soldier to Student: Easing the Transition of Service Members on Campus.* Washington DC: American Council on Education.

Davis, P. M. "Western Michigan University to Offer In-State Tuition to All Active Military Members." Kalamazoo, March 18, 2008. News Archive (blog), http://blog.mlive.com/kzgazette/2008/03/western_michigan_university_wi.html.

Frantz, S., and Asher, G. 2009. *Supporting Veterans in the Classroom. Minnesota State Colleges and Universities.* Little Falls, MN: PaperClip Communications.

KMI Media Group. 2009. 3rd Annual Guide to Military-Friendly Colleges & Universities. *Military Advanced Education* 4(6), 65.

Roland, C. 2007. WMU News Archives. Kalamazoo: Western Michigan University, May 2. Retrieved July 16, 2010, from http://www.wmich.edu/wmu/news/2007/09/033.html.

Schupp, J. 2009. *Supportive Education for the Returning Veteran-SERV* (pp. 1–33). Atlanta: Cleveland State University.

Strickley, V. L. 2009. *Veterans on Campus.* Little Falls, MN: PaperClip Communications.

Student Affairs Leadership Council, eds. 2009. *From Military Service to Student Life: Strategies for Supporting Student Veterans on Campus.* Washington, DC: The Advisory Board Company.

Student Veterans of America (SVA). 2010. "Michigan SVA Chapters." Washington, DC: Student Veterans of America. Accessed July 15, 2010, http://www.studentveterans.org/chapters/search.php.

US Department of Veterans Affairs. "MI State Yellow Ribbon Program Information 2010–2011." Washington, DC: US Department of Veterans Affairs, 2010. Accessed July 15, 2010, http://www.gibill.va.gov/gi_bill_info/ch33/YRP/2010/states/mi.htm.

Victory Media Inc. 2010. "Military Friendly Schools." Pittsburgh: Victory Media Inc. Accessed August 18, 2010, http://www.militaryfriendlyschools.com/search/profile.aspx?id=200004.

Western Michigan University (WMU). 2009. "Registered Student Information by Population." Kalamazoo: Western Michigan University.

Western Michigan University (WMU). 2010. "Registered Student Information by Veteran Type." Kalamazoo: Western Michigan University.

Wounded Warrior Project. 2010. Accessed January 31, 2010, http://www.woundedwarriorproject.org/.

TRACEY L. MOON *is the director of the Office of Military and Veterans Affairs at Western Michigan University.*

GERALDINE A. SCHMA *is a retired military advocate from the Advocacy Office for Transfer Students and Military Affairs, and the coordinator of the Veterans Transition Program of the Student Veterans of America.*

New Directions for Higher Education • DOI: 10.1002/he

8

*Combining university health centers and campus recreation and wellness centers into one facility is a new trend in collaborative facility design.*

# A Collaborative Approach to College and University Student Health and Wellness

*Darren S. Fullerton*

As colleges and universities around the country face extreme financial pressures, they also face mounting public expectations to improve and increase the quality and number of services they provide to their students. Some of these expectations include the presumption that the institutions will offer quality health care, fitness, and wellness services to complement the total student experience. One recent avenue used for addressing this expectation has been the collaborative enterprise between university health centers and university recreation and wellness centers and programs. Comprehensive student recreation and wellness centers have become a major component on today's college and university campuses. Universities expect these facilities to provide the "wow factor" for students; nevertheless, most traditional health centers have been viewed as a place to be avoided, unless the student is ill or injured.

One viable strategy for combating this economic downturn is to encourage internal collaboration between student health centers and their campus wellness, recreation, and fitness counterparts. This collaboration can provide opportunities for these entities to develop programs, services, and facilities that will better serve their students' total well-being in these financially challenging times.

## Barriers to Effectively Supporting Students

University departments within student affairs contribute to the overall personal development and learning of students by offering a wide array of high quality, comprehensive programs, services, and events in a supportive campus

New Directions for Higher Education, no. 153, Spring 2011 © Wiley Periodicals, Inc.
Published online in Wiley Online Library (wileyonlinelibrary.com) • DOI: 10.1002/he.427

environment. These student affairs programs and services are typically student-centered and provide a bridge to the academic mission of the university. Unfortunately, the higher education system in the United States may have contributed to many of its own major challenges, one of these being the notion that colleges and universities operate above and apart from the communities in which they are located. As Rudolph (1990) described it, "The establishment of Harvard University in 1636 (America's oldest university), was a planting of piety and intellect into the wilderness" (p. 3). For decades, universities (meaning faculty and staff) have seen themselves as the knights protecting the ivory tower. "Universities promoted themselves as elite bastions of information and knowledge" (Martin, Smith, and Phillips, 2005, p. 3). Even today we use the terms "town and gown" to describe the university's relationship with the community.

## Focused Programming Needs

Unfortunately, this separatist attitude has not only affected our community relationships, but also has carried over into many of the daily internal university operations. Various departments and divisions are constantly competing for rapidly disappearing operational budget dollars. This focus on finances alone has encouraged many departments to develop an attitude of isolationism. In today's financially challenged environment, many university departments and programs are presenting themselves as being so unique and specialized that sharing facilities and service functions is no longer a viable option. Unfortunately, this is not a new trend. Academic, athletic, health, recreation, and support service departments have been fighting for their share of facilities, finances, staff, and prestige for over a century. For example, ever since Rutgers defeated Princeton in the first intercollegiate football game in 1869, athletic facilities have played an integral part of the entire college campuses landscape (US Census Bureau, 2006). Additional evidence of this practice was shown in early 1928, with the construction of the intramural sports building on the campus of the University of Michigan. This building was one of the first facilities dedicated solely to recreational sports (Boger, 2008). Such facilities help strengthen the theory that to improve our programs and services, we need to separate and to specialize. Theories of specialization have led many college and university programs and departments to develop practices of poor internal communication, fostering a general lack of collaboration and cooperation with other divisions or units on campus. These practices can often create a campus atmosphere that is not supportive of the total development of the student. Today when we examine traditional college and university health centers, we find that they primarily focus on the treatment of physical illnesses, and the recreation and wellness centers primarily focus on physical fitness and well-being aspects (Neilson, Kotter, Padilla, Pennington, Pertofsky, Quirolgico, and Keeling, 2004).

## Establishing Partnerships

In a 2009 survey by the Association of Academic Health Centers, 89 percent of the responding academic health centers had established partnerships with community health centers (Brutger, 2010). University health centers value these types of community partnerships to supplement the services and programs that need to be offered to their students. Indeed, a web-based survey of wellness representatives at 241 colleges and universities in the nine states that make up the Central District Association of the American Alliance for Health, Physical Education, Recreation, and Dance, reported that 64.7 percent of two-year institutions and 78.9 percent of four-year institutions had a wellness program. In addition, 68.6 percent of two-year and 84.0 percent of four-year institutions reported having a dedicated wellness center (Strand, Egeberg, and Mozumdar, 2010). This survey highlights the prevalence of wellness centers and wellness programming on college and university campuses. Both of these surveys indicate that each of these student service areas are vital to student life on campus and that each of these service areas is already looking outside of its unit for cooperative partnerships. Collaboration could provide a multitude of opportunities for these entities to develop programs, services, and facilities to better serve students.

## Collaborative Services

Comprehensive health planning is not a new issue. Over 60 years ago, the World Health Organization defined health as "The state of complete physical, mental and social well-being and not merely the absence of disease or infirmity" (World Health Organization, 1948, p. 1). In addition, for years, education professionals and health professionals have advocated a direct relationship between students' general health and well-being and their academic success (Neilson, et al. 2004). With this in mind, many universities are constructing or remodeling facilities to combine state-of-the-art student recreation and fitness centers with university health centers, thus creating a one-stop shop for their students' health, wellness, and fitness needs.

To view examples of this trend, one can look to the 2009 and 2010 *Athletic Business* Magazine's "Architectural Showcase" special issues. In the 2009 edition, five of the twenty-two projects were identified as collegiate student recreation facilities (over 22 percent), including a prominent student health center facility (Athletic Business Editors, 2009). In the 2010 Showcase, six of the twenty-one projects were identified as collegiate student recreation facilities (over 28 percent), including a student health center facility (Athletic Business Editors, 2010). Another source for review is the 2008 National Intramural–Recreational Sports Association facilities survey. This survey, based on data collected from member and non-member colleges and universities, identified institutions that would be involved in capital projects from 2008 through 2013. Out of 179 colleges or universities that

### Table 8.1. Opportunities for Student Health and Recreation Collaboration

| | |
|---|---|
| Aromatherapy | Cholesterol screenings |
| Blood pressure checks | Health workshops |
| Flu shots | Immunizations |
| Drug and alcohol prevention | Social issues awareness |
| Diabetes screenings | Programs for the physically challenged |
| Nutrition education | Smoking cessation clinics |
| Stress management | Sexually transmitted disease education |
| Weight loss counseling | Eating disorder management |
| Depression treatment | Sleep disorder treatment |
| Exercise injury prevention | Healthy lifestyle programs |
| Wellness education | Mentor programs |
| Safety clinics | Ergonomic workshops |
| Informal fitness | Healthy relationships |
| Individual fitness programs | Preventative health services |
| Fitness & wellness trainers | Label reading workshops |
| Mental health services | Outdoor recreation |
| Massage | Child care services |

This list was compiled from various postings in *Athletic Business*, *American School and University*, and the National Intramural–Recreational Sports Association websites.

responded, 12 universities (6.7 percent) indicated that they were constructing some type of collaborative facility that included recreation/wellness programs and student health services (National Intramural– Recreational Sports Association, 2008).

Combining university health centers with campus recreation and wellness centers allows these student service programs to expand out of their individual departmental silos and offer health, wellness, and fitness programs that are truly comprehensive in nature. Although each of these student support areas has been very successful in reaching out to a select group of students, by combining these programs, facilities, and services under one roof, universities can reach a broader student base and provide a wide range of specialized services (see Table 8.1).

## Successful Partnerships

Collaborative programs benefit from cooperative programming opportunities and resources. Student recreation centers have typically been viewed as an aid in the university's recruitment, retention efforts, and overall quality of students' campus experience. Student health centers have primarily dealt with the treatment of illness and injuries, preventing illness or disease, and depending upon the program, might offer services that include psychological, social, behavioral, and emotional counseling.

One example would be at Missouri Southern State University (MSSU) in Joplin, Missouri. In September 2009, MSSU opened the Willcoxon Student Health Center, which is located inside the newly constructed Beimdiek Student Recreation Center. This facility is also home to the Freeman Wellness Testing Center, which is named for Freeman Health Systems, Inc., a local hospital system providing comprehensive health care and behavioral health services for the people of Southwest Missouri. The Freeman Wellness Testing Center focuses on Lifestyle Management, offering a computerized fitness assessment system that is used for measuring weight, body fat, blood pressure, heart rate, flexibility, and strength. The Wellness Center also offers fitness profile software to provide medical grade, interactive fitness assessments. In addition, this center is also home to a therapeutic aqua-massage treatment center. These items provide a nonthreatening approach to wellness and fitness that can supplement the services provided by the Willcoxon Health Center. By combining these facilities, MSSU not only improved the physical location of the Health Center, but it has also provided a variety of service opportunities, including enhancing interdepartmental communication, offering professionally conducted health fairs, and providing ongoing accessible health and fitness assessments conducted by professional medical staff. This partnership also allowed the medical team to utilize the fitness and wellness equipment and certified personal training staff from the Recreation Center to assist patients who might need to start a rehabilitation or physical fitness program. Due to this collaboration, the Willcoxon Health Center saw a 12-percent overall increase in the number of patient visits for the 2009–2010 academic year. It also saw a 13.75-percent increase in medical prescriptions, and a 90-percent increase in patients in the women's clinic preventative services. This is in contrast to the previously reported annual average of 1-percent to 2-percent increase per year (Dipley and Hosp, 2010).

Other examples of such centers include (1) the University of Colorado Denver Anschutz Medical Campus, which will offer a healthful food café/bistro and a healthful food market, while still enhancing student fitness, health, research, and lifestyle management; (2) South Dakota State University's Wellness and Student Health Center, which offers the convenience of an on-site pharmacy; and (3) the University of Nevada, Las Vegas Student Recreation and Wellness Center, which focuses on prevention, assessment, and educational opportunities (see Table 8.2).

## Sustainability

Even though colleges and universities are seeing very difficult financial times, many of them are still developing these types of projects. These recreation and health centers are deemed as necessary tools for competing in the recruitment war, in which many institutions find themselves.

New Directions for Higher Education • DOI: 10.1002/he

## Table 8.2. Colleges and Universities with Collaborative Facilities

Akron General Health & Wellness Center
Bradley University, Markin Family Student Recreation Center
Butler University (Indiana)
Florida State University
Long Island University in New York
Longwood University
Macalester College, The Leonard Center
Mayo Clinic Dan Abraham Healthy Living Center
Midwestern State University, The Bruce & Graciela Redwine Student Recreation Center
Minnesota State University–Moorhead, Dragon Wellness Center
Missouri Southern State University, Beimdiek Recreation Center
Oregon Health & Science University
Penn State University–Harrisburg
Queen's University
South Dakota State University, Wellness & Student Health Center
University of California–Berkeley
University of California–Merced, Joseph E. Gallo Recreation and Wellness Center
University of Nevada, Las Vegas Student Recreation & Wellness Center
University of North Carolina at Asheville
University of South Carolina Upstate
University of Southern Mississippi
University of Texas at San Antonio, Recreation & Wellness Center
Wartburg College, Waverly Community Wellness Center
Western Kentucky University
Xavier University

This list was compiled from various postings in *Athletic Business, American School and University*, and the National Intramural–Recreational Sports Association Survey.

According to the National Intramural–Recreational Sports 2008 Facilities survey, 174 colleges and universities were involved in 219 facility construction, expansion, and/or renovation projects. These campuses have a combined enrollment of 2.5 million students. The facilities represented in that report are expected to serve 1.87 million students each year. The average project expenditure according to the survey was $20.7 million (National Intramural–Recreational Sports Association, 2008).

Direct collaboration and cooperation between recreation and health centers provide colleges and universities with the opportunity to reach a multitude of their students with a focus on preventative fitness/wellness, instead of waiting for the students to seek treatment for an already developed illness, disease, or injury. In addition, the goal for many of these collaborative facilities is to provide opportunities that will foster the development of individual responsibility and the formation of lifelong healthy habits for the students. Jack Patton of RDG Planning and Design states, "This multidisciplinary approach and broader treatment options dovetail perfectly with the services provided by campus recreation professionals, who can leverage their specialized knowledge and resources to provide maximum therapeutic value for students. For campus healthcare providers, a merger provides staff and patients with immediate access to athletic or intramural activity spaces, larger physical therapy facilities and significantly larger fitness and weight rooms, thus reinforcing their programs and the benefits of lifelong activity and exercise" (2009, p. 28).

Additionally, this model can include the programming and specific service opportunities for specific groups of students, including those with special needs and nontraditional students. At times, both of these groups of students feel excluded from the services and programs offered by traditional recreational and health facilities. Collaborative facilities can provide a variety of appropriate, available services in an open and nonthreatening way. Programs and services that focus on their total well-being provide these students with an opportunity to pursue different areas of health and fitness without the stigma that they are being put on display. Many of these facilities offer specialized classes, screenings, and orientation programs that can accommodate the various needs of these students.

## Additional Opportunities

We examined a sustainable model for effective collaboration. The question is, "How can universities use this model to expand beyond the recreation and health center example?" University officials need to look beyond the individual department or college level to examine ways in which we could improve student success. Can administrators take our recreation/health model and expand it to include academic health and wellness students? It is easy to imagine health and wellness majors working in conjunction with the wellness testing labs, or implementing educational components for the health centers at these universities. What about areas such as nursing, dental hygiene, or respiratory therapy? Could these units also be brought into collaborative agreements?

Once an institution has started the review process, it can quickly start to visualize other potential university collaborations. Many universities are already looking at combining their first-year experience programs with long-standing support areas such as advising, disabilities services, tutoring, and the federal trio support programs to create a unified student success center. Can this synergy continue by combining other areas? Possible partnerships could include financial aid and the bursar's office, career services and alumni services, admissions and financial aid, or human resources and student employment. Universities are asking a variety of questions that impact how we serve students. Questions that should come to the forefront of these discussions include, "Can we enhance service, reduce costs, or improve efficiencies?"

New Directions for Higher Education • DOI: 10.1002/he

Once university administrators start examining these service issues from the service perspective, the possibilities for collaborative agreements on their respective campuses are greatly expanded.

## Conclusion

Currently, a wealth of anecdotal evidence suggests the trend of constructing a wellness and health center is rapidly gaining acceptance. The construction and design of these collaborative facilities will continue to grow as colleges and universities strive to provide the level of service and commitment that students and parents expect in an institution of higher education.

This is only the beginning of collaborative programs and services. The current national economic climate must be viewed as the "new financial reality." As progressive educators, we must strive to find more effective means of serving the needs of our students. Collaborative programs and facilities can provide a variety of appropriate, integrated services in an open and nonthreatening way to a wide variety of students. This will allow universities to focus on student success and development, while providing students with expanded services and facilities.

## References

Athletic Business Editors. 2009. "Architectural Showcase," special issue. *Athletic Business*, 33(6). Retrieved May 25, 2010, from http://www.athleticbusiness.com/galleries/ArchitecturalShowcase.aspx.

Athletic Business Editors. 2010. "Architectural Showcase," special issue. *Athletic Business*, 34(6), 32–177.

Boger, C.T. 2008. "Trends in Collegiate Recreational Sports Facilities." *The Sports Journal*, 11(4). Accessed May 27, 2010, http://www.thesportjournal.org/article/trends-collegiate-recreational-sports-facilities.

Brutger, R. D. *Academic Health Centers and Community Health Centers: The Landscape of Current Partnerships Association of Academic Health Centers*. Washington, DC: The Association of Academic Health Centers, 2010. Retrieved June 15, 2010, from http://www.aahcdc.org/policy/reddot/AAHC_Community_Health_Centers_The_Landscape.pdf.

Dipley, J., and Hosp, P. July 2010. "Willcoxon Health Center Annual Report." In *Student Affairs Annual Report*. Joplin: Missouri Southern State University.

Martin, L. L., Smith, H., and Phillips, W. 2005. "Bridging 'Town & Gown' Through Innovative University-Community Partnerships." *The Innovation Journal: The Public Sector Innovation Journal*, 10(2), Article 20. Accessed June 19, 2010, http:// www.innovation.cc/volumes-issues/martin-u-partner4final.pdf.

National Intramural–Recreational Sports Association. *Collegiate Recreational Sports Facilities Construction Report 2008–2013*. Corvallis, OR: The National Intramural–Recreational Sports Association, 2008. Accessed May 31, 2010, from http://www.nirsa.org/AM/Template.cfm?Section=Research_Central&Template=/MembersOnly.cfm&NavMenuID=828&ContentID=11331&DirectListComboInd=D.

Neilson, S., Kotter, M., Padilla, R., Pennington, K., Pertofsky, C., Quirolgico, R., and Keeling, R. 2004. *Leadership for a Healthy Campus: An Ecological Approach for Student*

*Success*. Washington, DC: The National Association of Student Personnel Administrators.

Patton, J. 2009. "Healthy Relationships." *Athletic Business*, 33(12), 26–32.

Rudolph, F. 1990. *The American College and University*. Athens: University of Georgia Press.

Strand, B. N., Egeberg, J., and Mozumdar, A. 2010. "The Prevalence and Characteristics of Wellness Programs and Centers at Two-Year and Four-Year Colleges and Universities." *Recreational Sports Journal*, 34, 45–57.

US Census Bureau. 2006. "First College Football Game." *BNET US Newswire*, November 5. Accessed June 19, 2010, http://www.prnewswire.com/news-releases/us-census-bureau-daily-feature-for-nov-6-69346897.html.

World Health Organization. 1948. *Constitution of the World Health Organization*. Accessed May 31, 2010, http://apps.who.int/gb/bd/PDF/bd47/EN/constitution-en.pdf.

DARREN S. FULLERTON *is the Interim Vice President for Student Affairs at Missouri Southern State University.*

# INDEX

# NEW DIRECTIONS FOR HIGHER EDUCATION

# ORDER FORM SUBSCRIPTION AND SINGLE ISSUES

## DISCOUNTED BACK ISSUES:

Use this form to receive 20% off all back issues of *New Directions for Higher Education*.
All single issues priced at **$23.20** (normally $29.00)

| TITLE | ISSUE NO. | ISBN |
|-------|-----------|------|
| _____ | _____ | _____ |
| _____ | _____ | _____ |
| _____ | _____ | _____ |

*Call 888-378-2537 or see mailing instructions below. When calling, mention the promotional code JBNND to receive your discount. For a complete list of issues, please visit www.josseybass.com/go/ndhe*

## SUBSCRIPTIONS: (1 YEAR, 4 ISSUES)

☐ New Order     ☐ Renewal

| | | |
|---|---|---|
| U.S. | ☐ Individual: $89 | ☐ Institutional: $259 |
| CANADA/MEXICO | ☐ Individual: $89 | ☐ Institutional: $299 |
| ALL OTHERS | ☐ Individual: $113 | ☐ Institutional: $333 |

*Call 888-378-2537 or see mailing and pricing instructions below.*
*Online subscriptions are available at www.onlinelibrary.wiley.com*

## ORDER TOTALS:

Issue / Subscription Amount: $ _____

Shipping Amount: $ _____
*(for single issues only – subscription prices include shipping)*

**Total Amount: $ _____**

| SHIPPING CHARGES: | |
|---|---|
| First Item | $5.00 |
| Each Add'l Item | $3.00 |

*(No sales tax for U.S. subscriptions. Canadian residents, add GST for subscription orders. Individual rate subscriptions must be paid by personal check or credit card. Individual rate subscriptions may not be resold as library copies.)*

## BILLING & SHIPPING INFORMATION:

☐ **PAYMENT ENCLOSED:** *(U.S. check or money order only. All payments must be in U.S. dollars.)*

☐ **CREDIT CARD:**  ☐ VISA  ☐ MC  ☐ AMEX

Card number _____ Exp. Date_____

Card Holder Name_____ Card Issue # _____

Signature _____ Day Phone_____

☐ **BILL ME:** *(U.S. institutional orders only. Purchase order required.)*

Purchase order # _____
Federal Tax ID 13559302 • GST 89102-8052

Name_____

Address_____

Phone_____ E-mail_____

Copy or detach page and send to:  **John Wiley & Sons, PTSC, 5th Floor**
**989 Market Street, San Francisco, CA 94103-1741**

Order Form can also be faxed to:  **888-481-2665**

PROMO JBNND

# Statement of Ownership

Statement of Ownership, Management, and Circulation (required by 39 U.S.C. 3685), filed on OCTOBER 1, 2010 for NEW DIRECTIONS FOR HIGHER EDUCATION (Publication No. 0271-0560), published Quarterly at Wiley Subscription Services, Inc., at Jossey-Bass, 989 Market St., San Francisco, CA 94103.

The names and complete mailing addresses of the Publisher, Editor, and Managing Editor are: Publisher, Wiley Subscription Services Inc., A Wiley Company at San Francisco, 989 Market St., San Francisco, CA 94103-1741; Editor, Martin Kramer, 2807 Shasta Road, Berkekey, CA 94708; Managing Editor, None.

NEW DIRECTIONS FOR HIGHER EDUCATION is a publication owned by Wiley Subscription Services, Inc. The known bondholders, mortgagees, and other security holders owning or holding 1% or more of total amount of bonds, mortgages, or other securities are (see list).

| | Average No. Copies Each Issue During Preceding 12 Months | No. Copies Of Single Issue Published Nearest To Filing Date (Summer 2010) |
|---|---|---|
| 15a. Total number of copies (net press run) | 966 | 897 |
| 15b. Legitimate paid and/or requested distribution (by mail and outside mail) | | |
| 15b(1). Individual paid/requested mail subscriptions stated on PS form 3541 (include direct written request from recipient, telemarketing, and Internet requests from recipient, paid subscriptions including nominal rate subscriptions, advertiser's proof copies, and exchange copies) | 413 | 385 |
| 15b(2). Copies requested by employers for distribution to employees by name or position, stated on PS form 3541 | 0 | 0 |
| 15b(3). Sales through dealers and carriers, street vendors, counter sales, and other paid or requested distribution outside USPS | 0 | 0 |
| 15b(4). Requested copies distributed by other mail classes through USPS | 0 | 0 |
| 15c. Total paid and/or requested circulation (sum of 15b(1), (2), (3), and (4)) | 413 | 385 |
| 15d. Nonrequested distribution (by mail and outside mail) | | |
| 15d(1). Outside county nonrequested copies stated on PS form 3541 | 33 | 33 |
| 15d(2). In-county nonrequested copies stated on PS form 3541 | 0 | 0 |
| 15d(3). Nonrequested copies distributed through the USPS by other classes of mail | 0 | 0 |
| 15d(4). Nonrequested copies distributed outside the mail | 0 | 0 |
| 15e. Total nonrequested distribution (sum of 15d(1), (2), (3), and (4)) | 33 | 33 |
| 15f. Total distribution (sum of 15c and 15e) | 446 | 418 |
| 15g. Copies not distributed | 520 | 479 |
| 15h. Total (sum of 15f and 15g) | 966 | 897 |
| 15i. Percent paid and/or requested circulation (15c divided by 15f times 100) | 93.1% | 92.1% |

I certify that all information furnished on this form is true and complete. I understand that anyone who furnishes false or misleading information on this form or who omits material or information requested on this form may be subject to criminal sanctions (including fines and imprisonment) and/or civil sanctions (including civil penalties).

(signed) Susan E. Lewis, VP & Publisher-Periodicals